Blairsville Joint
Junior High School

WINGS OF AN EAGLE

WINGS OF AN EAGLE

The Story of Michelangelo

by ANNE MERRIMAN PECK

with FRANK and DOROTHY GETLEIN

ILLUSTRATED BY LILI RÉTHI, F.R.S.A.

Hawthorn Books, Inc.   *Publishers*   *New York*

FIRST PRINTING

H–9408

WINGS OF AN EAGLE

CONTENTS

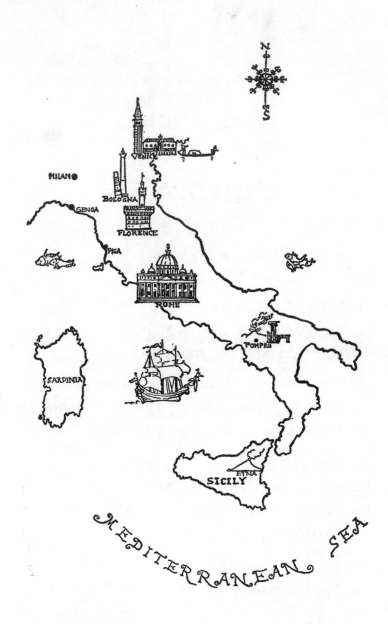

CHAPTER 1

A BOY IN FLORENCE

As the rising sun touched with light the tiled roofs
and church towers of the ancient city of Florence, a
boy slipped out the doorway of a tall stone house in
a shadowy street. He was a thin boy with broad
shoulders and a shock of dark hair. Looking up from
the shadows the boy's eyes noted with delight the
brightness of sunlit roof tops and the great dome of
the Cathedral that shone like a bubble against the pure
blue Italian sky.

Suddenly a deep-toned clamor of bells broke out

9

from numerous churches, calling the faithful to early Mass. Flights of doves and swallows, frightened by the noise, soared into the sky from their nests in the towers.

The boy drew in his breath. *"Bella, bellissima,"* he murmured; how beautiful were the swooping birds, the bells, the stone buildings.

The slight figure looked small and lonely in the dark street, and lonely he was, this boy whose name was Michelangelo de Buonarroti-Simoni. Only recently his father, Lodovico de Buonarroti-Simoni, had brought him to Florence to live in the family home with the brothers he hardly knew.

This was the beginning of an unhappy time for Michelangelo, who had passed his babyhood and early childhood with a warm-hearted stonecutter's family on a farm owned by Lodovico in the country near Florence. When Michelangelo was born on March 6, 1475, his father had a temporary position as mayor of a small town, Caprese. Since his frail mother could not take care of the baby, Lodovico had sent him to be nursed by the wife of the stonecutter at Settignano. Occasionally his parents came to the farm, but Michelangelo's mother died before long. He did not remember much about her. Lodovico remarried and moved to Florence where other sons were born.

The boy who had watched the flight of birds above the roof tops wandered on through the streets, now stirring with early morning activities. He thought back with homesick longing to the childhood at Settignano. He remembered the lovely countryside of olive groves and vineyards where he had run with the stonecutter's sons, and the big yard where huge blocks of marble and other fine stone were chiseled and shaped. He had watched the blocks loaded on oxcarts to be sent to the city of Florence for the building of churches and palaces.

He had played with marble chips and watched the men at work. The noise of hammer and chisel striking stone, the shouts and songs of the men as they worked in a cloud of marble dust were happy sounds to the boy. He was fascinated by the bow-shaped vibrating drill with which workers split hard blocks of marble. When he saw the glistening white of the split pieces he stooped to touch the smooth, cool stone.

As soon as childish hands could hold hammer and chisel, the stonecutter allowed his boys and Michelangelo to learn to manage the tools and chip at blocks. They watched the men test the quality of stone by running their hands over the surface. Soon the boy was learning that skill too. He came to know the quality of marble by the sense of touch. From these experiences Michelangelo learned to love stone, and the desire to hew shapes from the blocks became part of his very being.

11

The lonesome boy turned back from his morning ramble to his father's house, thinking miserably that happy childhood was over. He was an outsider in the household with his stern father, a stepmother, and brothers who looked down on him and called him a peasant. His older brother, Lionardo, was planning a religious vocation in the Church. The father did not object to that, but he intended to have the younger ones educated to become good merchants. Buonarroto, Giovansimoni, and Sigismondo were easygoing boys, too young as yet to have ambitions. Only Michelangelo resisted his father's plans for his future. He liked the working people he had lived with. He enjoyed working with his hands cutting stone. Already the desire to be an artist was in his heart. The last thing he wanted was to be a city merchant.

That morning when he entered his father's room, Lodovico looked up from his account books and said sharply, "So! You have returned from idling in the streets. This must stop, Michelangelo. You are ten years old; it is time you began an education befitting a son of the Buonarroti family. I shall send you to the grammar school of Messer Francesco da Urbino."

Michelangelo faced his father with stubborn resistance in every line of his body. "Father, school is a waste of time for me. I don't want to spend my days writing in account books and handling money. I must be an artist, and I must begin to learn how to draw." The boy remembered that he had loved to draw pictures on blocks with a piece of charcoal in the stone-cutter's yard.

Lodovico struck his fist on the table. "A Buonarroti become an artist! Impossible," he shouted. "A stone-cutter is nothing but a laborer, and a painter isn't much better. Painters live like vagabonds, they are not respected, they don't make money. The Buonar-rotis do not work with their hands like laborers."

Lodovico Buonarroti was a harsh, narrow-minded man with great pride of family. For generations the Buonarrotis had been respected merchants in Flor-ence and, although Lodovico was no longer wealthy, he stuck fiercely to his belief in their high position. He claimed aristocratic ancestry and boasted that for three hundred years no Buonarroti had gone hungry. Successful money-making was Lodovico's ideal of a proper, respected position.

Sparks of anger lit the boy's hazel eyes. "You and my uncles work with your hands doing sums and counting money. I shall use my hands to draw and carve marble. I shall be like the great artists of this city who *are* respected—they are highly honored."

Father and son faced each other in stubborn fury. For days the arguments went on, the uncles joining the father in their insistence on school. Michelangelo was helpless against them. He was only a child, sub-ject to his father's orders.

Reluctantly Michelangelo joined other boys in the grammar school of Messer Francesco da Urbino,

13

there to learn reading, writing, accounting, and perhaps a little Latin. In later life he was glad that he had learned to read the beautiful Italian language because of the inspiration he found in books and because of the ability he developed to write poetry himself. But in school the boy was rebellious. How could he be shut up in a dark room with musty books among boys he didn't care for when the whole wonderful city of Florence was around him to be explored?

Michelangelo took every opportunity to slip away from school to wander through the streets and the plazas, along the banks of the River Arno that flowed through the city with bridges across it. He studied the fishermen and the glittering fish piled in the market. He watched laden oxcarts drawn by great white oxen, the market women with baskets on their heads, or perhaps a cavalcade of young noblemen clattering through the street on handsome horses. His fingers itched to draw the people and animals, the activities in the streets. Whenever he could get possession of a sheet of paper and a pen, he hid himself in his room to make sketches.

At school his notebooks had sketches along the borders of pages, mingled with sums and rules of grammar. He dreamed over his books and could not put his mind on study. One day when he was supposed to be writing a lesson, but was drawing figures in action, a heavy hand fell on his shoulder.

14

"Wake up, boy, and get to work," the master said sternly. "This notebook is for lessons, not drawings. Pay attention to your work, Michelangelo." And he whacked the lad with his ruler.

This happened several more times. When Master Urbino reported to Michelangelo's father that his son was bright but would not study, the father raged at the news. He added a beating to the whacks received at school. It had no effect on the rebellious boy who continued to go his own way, absorbed in the wonders of Florence.

He lingered in the streets of the craftsmen—the weavers and dyers of fabrics, the metal workers, the stonecutters' shops. The clang and ring of hammers made him homesick for Settignano. He looked in at the studios of painters where young apprentices were drawing and preparing materials for the master painters. It was the practice at that period for young artists to learn their skills by working as apprentices in the studios of established painters. One day, at the studio of the famous painter Ghirlandaio, a young assistant noticed the shy boy standing in the doorway.

"Come in, friend," he said. "Mayhap you would like to see the studio. I am Francesco Granacci, assistant to Master Ghirlandaio."

"Thank you, Messer Granacci. I am Michelangelo Buonarroti, at your service."

"Oh, yes, I know who your father is. Come in, I

will show you what an apprentice has to learn in order to become a painter."

Michelangelo was taken through a large room with a long table down the middle. Here apprentices were copying drawings or enlarging sketches for the murals the master was designing. Francesco stopped beside a youth who was grinding a lump of scarlet pigment with pestle and mortar. "You see," he said, "the pigment must be ground into powder, then mixed with water for painting."

Michelangelo watched everything in the studio intently. Francesco recognized the spirit of a young artist in the boy's interest. He went with him to the street and said, "You might like to be an apprentice in our studio. Come again."

"I must be an artist," Michelangelo replied earnestly, "but my father forces me to go to school. I run away when I can, there is so much to see."

"I don't blame you," Francesco said with a laugh. "But I'll wager you wouldn't run away from the study of drawing."

Michelangelo gazed with admiration at this slender, attractive Florentine of nineteen years. To the boy he seemed a marvelous young man.

"I'll help you," Francesco said, responding to the admiration. "There is a lot to learn before you become an artist."

From that first meeting a firm friendship grew up

between the two youths. They made appointments to meet, sometimes at the studio, sometimes on the Cathedral steps. Francesco gave his friend paper, ink and pens, and loaned him masters' drawings from the studio to copy. These Michelangelo hid under the bed in the room he shared with his brother Buonarroto. This brother was the only one in the family who really loved the lonely boy. He admired Michelangelo and stood by him, helping to hide the drawings from their father.

Francesco and Michelangelo snatched every bit of spare time to continue their self-education among the works of art in churches and public buildings. Florence in the late fifteenth century was in the full glory of the Renaissance. This period was so called because it was a great rebirth of art, poetry and learning, a return to the classic arts of Greece and Rome. The Renaissance began in Italy and spread to other countries of Europe.

Italy, at that period, was not a nation as we know it today. It was a collection of city-states, generally ruled by powerful families of ancient nobility. Florence was a republic, governed by a body of citizens called the Signoria. Every phase of life, however, was dominated by the Medici, a family of wealthy, intelligent merchant princes. Lorenzo the Magnificent, head of the family when Michelangelo was young, was a great patron of the arts and a

17

They studied the carvings by Luca della Robbia.

scholar, as well as a wealthy banker and merchant, known throughout Italy. Florence was the richest and most populous of the city-states. Its merchants traded with all Italy and with other European countries. Besides its rich trade, the city was on the main routes of travel over most of Italy; particularly it was on the roads from north, east, and west that led to the city of Rome, the center of Christianity and the home of the Popes.

In their wanderings Michelangelo and Francesco studied masterpieces of painting, sculpture, and architecture. They marveled at the great dome of Il Duomo, the Cathedral designed by Brunelleschi. It was said that all the people of Tuscany could stand in the shadow of the mighty dome. Near the Cathedral was the campanile, the bell tower, designed by the great artist Giotto, with sculptured decorations by Andrea Pisano. The boys particularly admired the paintings of Giotto for the strong simplicity and spiritual feeling of his figures. Giotto was the true founder of Florentine art.

Within the Cathedral they studied choruses of singing boys carved in marble by Luca della Robbia. On the great doors of the Baptistry, modeled and cast in bronze by Lorenzo Ghiberti, Michelangelo studied intently the scenes from Scripture, modeled in relief. They were enclosed within borders of men, plants and animals, with the self-portrait of the sculptor himself in one of the figures.

The city was alive with great art. Michelangelo was inspired more by the sculpture than by the painting, but both students admired the delicate angels and Virgins painted by the gentle monk Fra Angelico, and the lovely Madonnas created by Fra Lippo Lippi. The churches were peopled with kings and prophets of the Old Testament, with Christ and his apostles, all carved in stone, cast in bronze or painted on the walls by glorious artists. Worshippers had the sacred stories of their religion around them in the churches.

The two young students would say to each other, "We are blessed to be living in Florence now." Not only did they have the art of the past to study, but new works of painting, sculpture, and architecture were constantly being produced. The wealth of the Church and of rich noblemen and merchants was spent to adorn churches with works of art. And Florence was the goal for the finest artists and scholars of Renaissance Italy.

It was not surprising that Michelangelo could not pay attention to his studies; the world outside the classroom was too absorbing. For three years the struggle went on. Every time his father found Michelangelo working on a drawing he snatched it and tore it up in a rage. Threats and punishment had no effect on the boy. His answer to all the storms was always, "I must be an artist."

At last, when Michelangelo was thirteen, Master

Urbino came to Lodovico Buonarroti to say that it was no use for his son to continue school. It was best to apprentice him to a painter, for he was determined to be an artist and his drawings showed promise. This was a hard blow for the father who thought art was an unworthy trade for a Buonarroti.

Francesco Granacci called on him to tell him that if he would apprentice Michelangelo to Ghirlandaio, in whose studio he worked, it would be of great benefit to the boy. Ghirlandaio was the most popular painter in Florence, high in favor with the powerful Medici family. Michelangelo would meet important people; he would become a famous artist himself.

Lodovico gave in at last. With a haughty air, as though conferring a favor, he asked Ghirlandaio to take his son into the studio as an apprentice. Ghirlandaio had seen the boy's drawings and knew he would be useful. He even consented, on Lodovico's insistence, to pay Michelangelo a small wage.

So it was that, at the age of thirteen, Michelangelo won his first battle in a life that would be full of conflicts. He was started on his lifelong urge to create beauty through art.

CHAPTER 2

THE APPRENTICE

In the church of Santa Maria Novella, tall scaffold-ings had been built against the walls in one chapel. Painters were at work on the platforms, rapidly brushing brilliant colors into wet plaster that had been smoothed on a section of the wall by an ap-prentice. In the body of the chapel students were running to and fro with palettes and cups of color for the painters. One apprentice was grinding color with pestle and mortar, while another was preparing

22

plaster for the wall. Still others were working on huge sheets of paper by which the designs would be transferred to the wall. Here Domenico Ghirlandaio was supervising work on the murals he had been commissioned to paint in their chapel by the wealthy Tornabuoni family. Into this busy scene Francesco Granacci led the excited Michelangelo on the first day of his apprenticeship.

"Everybody in the studio is working at the church these days," he told Michelangelo, "for the Master has begun painting the scenes on the walls. I am to work on painting today, but I will take you around and show you what to do."

The work was not new to Michelangelo for he had haunted the chapel many times when Francesco was helping there, watching each operation of the apprentices. He went to work with a will after Francesco had introduced him to the workers. He carried water to the plaster mixers; he carried brushes, palettes, and cups of color to the painters on scaffolds. Day after day passed while he concentrated on learning all the tasks expected of apprentices.

When one section of the wall was finished, the young students moved back to the studio in a jolly crowd, with their materials transported in a donkey cart. Drawings were to be prepared for the next section of the murals.

Ghirlandaio was working with "true fresco," the

23

favorite medium for murals at that period of the Renaissance, although some artists were painting with oils, especially for portraits or small altar pieces. Part of the schooling for the students in the Ghirlandaio workshop was to learn every step in the painting of frescoes.

The Master ordered Francesco to teach Michelangelo just how to mix the ingredients for the plaster ground, how to make the mixture the right consistency, and how to apply it to a wall in the studio yard. The boy watched his friend's work carefully. Then Francesco handed him a trowel and said, "Now spread the plaster on this piece of wall. Make it smooth and even."

When the surface was approved by Francesco he gave the boy a large sheet of paper with a man's figure drawn on it in chalk. Under instruction Michelangelo punched small holes along the lines of the drawing with a sharp pointed instrument. Then Francesco laid the sheet of paper on the wet plaster. He pounded the punched holes of the drawing with a small thin bag filled with powdered charcoal. When he pulled off the paper, the lines of the drawing were on the plaster in charcoal dots. Francesco took a piece of red chalk and joined the dots in firm lines.

"Now, you see, Michelangelo, that is how you transfer the large drawings to the walls. Next the colors are painted in before the plaster dries. In that way the color seeps through the plaster. It is not just on the surface, it is there to stay."

"*Mamma mia*," exclaimed Michelangelo. "Must I learn all these labors for painting frescoes? That's not what I'm here for. I want to draw and carve stone."

"Patience, boy. That will come in time. An artist must learn by practice every step, every technique of his trade in order to become a worthy master." Francesco laughed at his eager friend. "Tomorrow we'll put you at the drawing table."

Michelangelo joined the youths who were at work on drawings on the long table in the middle of the studio. They were merry, carefree young fellows, some older, some younger than he. Their work was done carefully and accurately under the sharp eye of the master painter, but they did not take it very seriously. They were learning a trade, while at the same time they intended to enjoy life.

The new apprentice was greeted with good-natured teasing which he could not take in the right spirit. He was too shy, too serious to give back the jokes, and he soon became the object of tricks such as boys everywhere will play on a new member of their gang. Michelangelo's hot temper flared up, but he kept his mouth shut and went on grimly with his drawing. When, after work hours, the boys trooped off to have fun in the town, they did not ask him to go with them. Francesco tried to persuade the lad to go out with him. "We'll see if there isn't a parade going on, or we can sit on the Cathedral steps to watch the people as they go by."

Michelangelo shook his head. "I don't have time for people and fun—I have so much to learn." Nevertheless he could not help feeling lonely and left out. He did not know how to make friends.

Day after day he worked with concentration, copying drawings from the studio collection of master work. This he loved; it was work he had done surreptitiously at home when Francesco brought him drawings. He was learning actions and gestures of men and women, facial expressions, perspective, and the folds of drapery. He was particularly interested in a print of a drawing by Martin Schongauer, a German. It had a rude strength very different from the grace and sweetness of Italian drawing. He copied the print and it influenced his style of drawing. When he came to create art of his own, he combined some of the harsh power of the North with the grace of Italy.

Ghirlandaio, like every mural painter, started a project by painting a small model to scale of the designs to go on the walls with figure grouping, landscape, color, and details. Sometimes the small paintings were done in an architectural framework such as they would have on the wall when finished. The model for the Biblical scenes to be painted in the church of Santa Maria Novella stood on the long

26

work table. Some students were making sketches from figures in the model, some were enlarging small drawings from the scenes to a large scale to fit the walls. These drawings on huge sheets of paper were called cartoons.

Master Ghirlandaio was pleased with Michelangelo's sketches and often stopped to watch the new apprentice. This boy with his skill in drawing would be useful for work on the cartoons. So the young artist was promoted to the more important work. He was shown how to calculate proportions of figures, to enlarge them to the right scale for the walls.

For the new apprentice this cartoon drawing was work that aroused his imagination and restless spirit. What satisfaction to draw in the large figures with free sweeps of the chalk, to emphasize action and gestures! His imagination thought of compositions on a large scale, full of energy. Not for him the dainty painting of landscapes or rich costumes and flowery decoration.

Yet he had to submit to such ornamental jobs very soon. The midsummer festival of Saint John's Day was approaching, a time when all the people plunged into days and nights of carnival. The wealthy families were commissioning the best painters in the studios to design carnival floats, banners, and costumes for the parades. All the apprentices at the Ghirlandaio studio were busy composing and painting decorations.

27

Michelangelo grumbled to Francesco, "Why should serious artists be asked to design and paint such frivolous fancies?"

Master Ghirlandaio, who overheard the remark, said firmly, "Listen, my son. Never refuse a commission, never send a customer away unsatisfied. An artist, if he is going to succeed, must paint what people want. Paint things well, but don't scorn the demand, even though it is for nothing more than to paint a wreath of flowers around a lady's basket."

In fact, it was their skill at such pretty designing that had helped to bring wealth to Domenico and David Ghirlandaio and had won them their name, for Ghirlandaio meant "garland maker." The Florentine ladies were excessively fond of ornate frills and fancies and gorgeous costumes. Any painter who could portray their brocades and silks, their furs, the jewels around their necks and on headdresses with realistic beauty was sure to win commissions from them.

For the few days of joyous festival the population lived in the streets day and night. Happy crowds of fantastically costumed people danced beside the processions of floats on which rode men and women attired like pagan gods and goddesses. The crowd exchanged gifts; they laughed at shows of wild beasts or performances of jugglers.

The boys from the studio, including Michelangelo and Francesco, roamed the city with sketchbooks in

They stopped to sketch the joyous crowd.

hand, enjoying the excitement, color, noise and music, feasting with the crowd on food and wine provided free by the Medici family. They stopped to sketch a couple of fellows who were too joyful with their wine-drinking, or catch the actions of laughable masked characters who were performing like clowns. At night the city rang with song and the music of instruments, while fireworks spangled the sky. They watched circles of men and girls who were prancing around huge bonfires, sniffing the good smell of roasting oxen that was being cooked for colossal barbecues.

"Come on, Michelangelo," shouted Francesco, "get yourself a girl and join the fun." The other boys had caught partners and Francesco darted in, choosing a pretty girl, as they all danced around the fire. Michelangelo hung back. He was too self-conscious, too afraid of being laughed at, to prance around and kick up his heels like his companions. He stood alone in the shadows, watching and longing to join in, but he had lived shut up in himself too long to laugh and be foolish.

After the festival the Florentines settled down, while the young artists at the Ghirlandaio studio worked hard at the church of Santa Maria Novella. The murals were nearly finished. One day when the Master was out, Michelangelo stopped to watch the complicated scene of activity. He snatched a big sheet of paper and began to draw the scaffolding with the painters at work, the trestles below, and the crew of helpers on the floor busy with their various tasks. He was too absorbed to notice when Ghirlandaio returned and stopped beside him to look at the drawing. He took it up to study. Well, this young fellow was indeed observant and skillful, each detail was drawn to perfection. He thought, "This boy knows as much as I do." However, he returned the drawing with the brief remark, "Very good. Now get on with the work."

At last the scaffoldings were taken down. The walls were revealed, glowing with soft, rich colors in the graceful groups of figures against a background of charming Italian landscape. Francesco was excited as he and Michelangelo studied the paintings.

"Isn't it beautiful—look at the harmony of colors Ghirlandaio has developed, and the skill of the drawing. That is what I want, to become a master of fresco painting, and also of oil painting. You must admit, my friend, that fresco is a challenge. Every line, every brush stroke of color must go on the walls just right, for you can't change anything. You'd have to scrape off the plaster and start over again."

Michelangelo studied the pictures with keen eyes.

"Yes," he said slowly. "It is a challenge, but the painting is too flat to suit me; those figures don't have enough strength, and they are not my idea of the Biblical characters."

The Bible was the favorite reading of this serious boy who had grown up with the Christian principles and ceremonies of the Church, as was true of most young people. He knew the stories and personalities of the Old and New Testaments. The prophets and apostles in the frescoes wore the elaborate costumes of Florentines, and each Biblical personality was an exact portrait of a Tornabuoni or some other prominent Florentine. Even the Madonna had the face of a lovely Florentine lady.

"Ghirlandaio has painted Florence and its people, not the holy figures of the Bible," he said.

It was true that their master had a gift for portraiture, and no one thought it inappropriate that he had given the faces of Florentines to characters in Biblical scenes—in fact, the Florentines were pleased. At that time it was the custom to portray, somewhere in the composition of sacred paintings, the figures of the wealthy donors who had paid for the pictures.

Michelangelo shook his head. "Frescoes are not for me, nor is oil painting. It is too easy, too flat."

Francesco looked at the strong hands of his friend, with the sensitive fingers that were now clenched as though to grasp a tool.

"Ah, yes, I see you are still hankering after stone. Come, I'll show you something."

He led Michelangelo through the streets to the Monastery of San Marco and opened a door in a high wall. They stepped into a beautiful hidden garden. Michelangelo stopped short. *"Dio mio,"* he gasped. "What magnificence!"

Under the shade of trees and along the paths stood marble figures of antique Greek and Roman art— figures of gods and goddesses, youths in action, beautiful carved heads, or torsos that had lost head or arms.

Francesco explained, "This is the garden where Lorenzo the Magnificent places antique masterpieces he has bought and hasn't room for in the palace. The Medicis support the Monastery, you see, so Lorenzo may use the garden if he likes. The monks don't mind, most likely they enjoy the sculptures, even if they are pagan. This beautiful place is called the Garden of the Gods."

That first glimpse of the statuary garden brought Michelangelo to a turning point in his life. He had finished one year of his contract to Ghirlandaio and he was dissatisfied. To be sure, he had won some respect from his father because he brought him the florins of his small wages at regular intervals. He was contributing to the support of his family, but he was not doing the work he wanted. He was about fifteen, a young man by the standard of the times.

Michelangelo learned that Lorenzo the Magnificent had organized, in a building adjoining the garden, a school of sculpture with a fine sculptor, Master

33

Bertoldo, as teacher. Lorenzo wanted to restore the art of sculpture in Florence to its former glory. It became the consuming ambition of the young artist to join that studio.

Then, one day, Ghirlandaio announced to his apprentices that Lorenzo de' Medici had requested the masters of the painting studios to send their best students to the school of sculpture. The Master was not pleased with the request, which amounted to a command since the Medici wanted it. However, he saw a chance to pass on Michelangelo to another teacher. This young man was too unconventional, too violent in his emotions, too rebellious to fit in with the other students. Ghirlandaio told his students that he was sending Michelangelo and Francesco Granacci to the Bertoldo studio, and was releasing them from their contracts to him.

Michelangelo was overjoyed. At last he could learn to carve stone! He did not dare tell his father that he was to work under a sculptor; he merely said that he and Granacci were to be sent to make some drawings from the statuary in the Garden of the Gods. The lad with the sculptor's hands and the great dreams in his soul entered on the happiest period of his life.

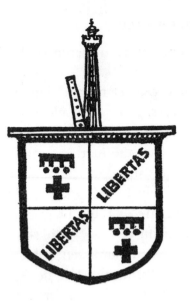

CHAPTER 3

IN THE MEDICI PALACE

Sunlight and shadow flickered over the marble figures standing in the Garden of the Gods. There were statues of pearly, gleaming marble, others that were stained and mellowed from having lain in the ground or under water until they were discovered, to be dug up and sold to Lorenzo de' Medici. In the garden there was a happy stir of young artists at work with laughter and chatter as they carried on their study in the big studio or were crouched with their

35

drawing papers before a statue or broken piece of sculpture.

Michelangelo was set to studying and drawing the sculptured figures. Now he could run his hands over the swelling muscles of a torso, feeling the movement before he translated the marble form into a drawing. Or he could study and draw the clear-cut features on the head of a lovely Greek goddess. At last he could realize the structure of the human body in sculpture as well as in drawings.

Nude figures had not been painted for about a thousand years. During the Middle Ages the churchmen, who were the principal employers of artists, ruled that figures in sacred paintings for churches must be clothed in flowing draperies. And Florentine artists of Michelangelo's time enjoyed painting with skill the beauty of silk, velvet, and jewels, so were glad to clothe their figures.

Donatello was the first sculptor of the Renaissance to create statues in the nude. The free spirit of Renaissance artists and poets adopted the Greek worship of physical perfection in the human form, and their magnificent sculptures were cherished. This feeling for physical beauty was one aspect of the rebirth of art that Michelangelo agreed with wholeheartedly.

These antique marbles, still so full of life, were his best friends in the garden, although he enjoyed some

36

of the gentler students. Francesco Granacci was always near him, modeling in clay or drawing with enthusiasm. Days in this place of art and beauty were happy ones, but at home Michelangelo was ignored by the family except for his brother Buonarroto. His father was furious when he finally learned that his son was working for a sculptor and not even earning a penny as he had in the painting studio; he was a stonecutter again! He left home early in the morning and lingered in the garden after the other students left to study the wonderful statues.

The impatient student learned that he would not yet be allowed to take chisel and hammer in hand to carve marble. Master Bertoldo told him he must draw constantly and study form before he could work on stone. The Master taught the eager youth to make an armature of wire for a figure, then mold clay over the frame to model the shape and movements of the body. In this way he learned to study small figures from every angle—front, back, and profile.

Master Bertoldo was an enthusiastic teacher, although he was a frail old man. His master had been Donatello, and to his mind this sculptor had attained a perfection in carving human figures from marble. Bertoldo insisted that his students observe every detail of Donatello's indication of structure, modeling of muscles, carving of hands and feet.

The old teacher was greatly interested in the in-

37

tense young student who was so absorbed in sculpture, and Michelangelo felt very close to his teacher whom he admired and respected. The day came when Master Bertoldo handed him hammer and chisel with the words, "Now, my boy, you shall learn to understand stone and create beauty from it."

Eagerly Michelangelo joined the group in the sculpture section of the big studio. They were learning to study the quality of a block of marble, to feel the shape of head or figure they might carve from it. Then, by practice with various tools, they learned to cut away the stone and bring into being the form they imagined within it. In this phase of his study Michelangelo was supremely happy.

Master Bertoldo often sent his students to draw from the frescoes of Masaccio in the church of the Carmine. This talented painter, who died young, had left unfinished frescoes that had a freedom and sculpturesque quality unlike the painting of other artists. These were paintings Michelangelo was glad to admire and copy. The figures were drawn vigorously but simply, rounded in modeling, emotional in expression. They seemed to have air around them. "If I could paint like that," Michelangelo thought, "I wouldn't hate fresco so much. They are something like sculpture."

In the garden Lorenzo de' Medici had placed a new acquisition, the carved head of a wicked, grinning old

38

faun. Michelangelo was fascinated by it; what expression in the laughing mouth, what an impish leer in the slanting eyes! He longed to copy it, but knew the Master would not permit this. There was a handy chunk of marble lying under some bushes in the rear of the garden. The young fellow took it and made a working place for himself back of the bushes where he would not be noticed. Early in the morning he sneaked into the garden and remained late in the afternoon to work on the carved head. The personality of the old faun was emerging from the block, and presently he became so absorbed that he worked all day on the head. Late in the afternoon, when he was polishing the finely carved features of his faun, he felt the presence of someone standing beside him. He looked up into the dark, compelling eyes of Lorenzo the Magnificent himself! Michelangelo gasped.

The great patron of the arts was a strong figure of a man, although far from handsome. He had a bad complexion, a lantern jaw, big nose, and lanky black hair. But when he smiled, the warmth of that smile and the friendliness in the dark eyes reassured the young artist.

"Well," said Lorenzo, "so you are copying my faun."

He took up the piece of marble to study it, noting the vigor of the carving, but he said no word of

39

praise. "My faun is old," he remarked, "and you have left him all his teeth. Don't you know that teeth fall out when one is old?" With that remark he walked away.

Michelangelo studied his work. True, the face did not look old enough. With his tools he knocked out one tooth, then another, and re-worked the whole mouth to make it look natural.

Lorenzo appeared again the next afternoon just as the young artist was putting the finishing touches on the head. Once more he said nothing in praise as he stooped to look at the carving.

"That is better. You have made the old creature's mouth very natural," he remarked. After studying the boy for a moment he asked, "Your father is Lodovico de Buonarroti, is he not? Will you tell him to come to the palace. I wish to speak with him."

With fear and anxiety in his heart, Michelangelo carried the message to his father that evening. Lodovico was overwhelmed. What had his crazy son been up to now—had he offended the great Medici? He did not like to be ordered to the palace, but a command from the Medici could not be ignored.

The next day Lodovico dressed in his best and went to the palace. His eyes fairly popped out as a guard led him through a great courtyard where sea captains, traders, and artists were gathered; then up a winding staircase and through lofty rooms that were a treasure house of painting, sculpture, and tapestries. So he came to the audience chamber and was admitted to Lorenzo's presence.

The great one wasted no time. "Buonarroti, I would like your son to come to the palace to live," said the most important man in Florence. "He has genius and I would like to help him become a great artist."

Trembling, Lodovico bowed low. "Your Magnificence, your commands must be obeyed, but I do not want my son to be a servant."

Lorenzo smiled. "Don't worry, Messer Lodovico. Your son will live as one of my family, he will eat at table with my family and friends. He will continue his work at the Bertoldo studio. What can I do for you in return for the loan of your son?"

Bowing his head Lodovico thought rapidly. He did not dare to ask for money. "There is a secretaryship open at the Customs office," he said hesitatingly.

The great man smiled at this modest request. "It shall be yours, but I am afraid you will never get rich. Tell Michelangelo to come to the palace."

When Master Bertoldo announced to the students that Michelangelo was to become a protegé of Lorenzo the Magnificent and was invited to live in the palace, they crowded around the embarrassed youth with excited congratulations. Francesco put his arm

41

Torregiano broke Michelangelo's nose.

around Michelangelo's shoulder. "How glad I am for you, my talented friend. Now you will have every opportunity to become a famous artist."

Only the student Torregiano, a big, aggressive, young man, did not congratulate his fellow student.

He had little talent but great ambition, and he was jealous of this honor conferred on the aloof, hard-working young artist.

When the students were busy that afternoon copying frescoes at the church of the Carmine, Torregiano picked a quarrel with Michelangelo, taunting him with words and jeers. He knew of the fellow's fiery temper, how he resented insults, and the youth reacted with angry words as he expected. Soon they came to blows, and in their struggle Torregiano smashed his fist into Michelangelo's face, breaking his nose. The students pushed the bully away with angry shouts, while Bertoldo staunched the bleeding and carried the injured boy to his own room in the palace, where he tended him until the nose healed. Michelangelo thus began his new life in a sad, fearful mood. He, a lover of beauty, would be disfigured for life, and he was too conscious of the blemish to respond to the people he met.

Lorenzo gave him attention and friendliness. He showed him some of the art treasures in the palace and introduced him to the Medici sons—Piero, Giovanni, and Giuliano. They were pleasure-loving youths, well educated, but lacking their father's fine mind.

Michelangelo gradually adjusted himself to life in the palace, finding release in his work at the studio. At night he joined the company of artists, scholars, and philosophers around the large, sumptuous dinner

43

table. Lorenzo, a man of democratic spirit, never arranged his table to have the most important people close to him. If distinguished visitors arrived first, they had the cherished seats, but if they were late, humble members of the company such as Michelangelo sat near their host.

Many of Lorenzo's regular guests were the most creative men in Italy, who lived in a villa at Fiesole, owned by Lorenzo, where they carried on studies in Greek thought and philosophy. The shy newcomer felt his mind expand as he listened with keen attention to the discussions, the like of which he had never heard.

One of the most famous of the poets and scholars was a young man, Poliziano, who was tutor to the Medici sons. He noticed the deep feeling in the eyes of the silent, awkward man and made friends with him. Soon they were close companions, spending many evenings in talk and reading. Poliziano introduced Michelangelo to Dante's great poetic work, *The Divine Comedy*. They read it together many times until this book, next to the Bible, was the constant source of inspiration to Michelangelo. The poet's dream journey through Purgatory, Hell, and Paradise roused a deep response in Michelangelo's religious spirit.

Entirely different was the reading by Poliziano from the works of Homer. The poet also related to

44

his young friend tales of Greek myths, of gods and goddesses, that helped him to understand the antique sculptures he admired so much.

As an adopted member of Lorenzo's family, Michelangelo was included in the extravagant parties of poetry, song, and merry-making that took place, generally in the gardens at Fiesole. Intense, serious and shy, he could not feel at home with the graceful, handsome Florentine youths and the perfumed, lovely girls he met. He dressed like the others in doublet and hose of rich colors, thanks to Lorenzo's generosity, but he did not look like them. Hard work chiseling stone had strengthened his broad shoulders and powerful hands. He was short and stocky, and his hazel eyes were the only light in his sober face. Sometimes the Medici sons invited him to join their hunting parties or other festivities, but he always refused.

To Lorenzo, his patron, the young artist gave complete loyalty and affection. This man of fine humane spirit had awakened his thinking and given him the opportunity to develop his art, which he thought of as a divine gift. He understood that Lorenzo was seeking the finest achievements of man to be accomplished through freedom of thought and feeling.

Freedom to enjoy beauty in every form was natural to his artistic spirit; he was tempted by the luxury and gaiety of Florentine life as any young man would be. He responded to the delight of song and poetry,

45

the admiration of physical beauty, but he felt that the Florentines were rejecting Christian principles. He was disturbed by the pagan spirit of many Florentine festivals. The conflict between sensuous pleasure and the love of God was intense in Michelangelo's spirit and was reflected in his work.

He was engaged on two relief carvings for Lorenzo. Relief is an art form somewhere between painting and sculpture. The figures are brought out of the stone, but are still attached to it. The scene appears to be almost on one plane, like a painting.

Michelangelo expressed his strong feeling for action and struggle in a carved relief called the Battle of the Centaurs, a story taken from Greek myth. The carving was a turmoil of conflict, of bodies struggling together, or wounded and collapsing, twisting and fighting.

He turned from this violent piece to the spiritual beauty of the Virgin and Child in a relief called the Madonna of the Stairs. His Virgin was not the sweet, delicate figure popular with Florentine painters but a strong, mature woman. She sits with the Child upon her lap, facing with calm sadness the future she has accepted, as she looks at a stairway where a figure is holding the shroud of Christ.

Lorenzo was greatly pleased with both reliefs and paid the young sculptor with a purse of gold florins. Now, thought Michelangelo, he would give his father

46

a prize he could appreciate when he made his next visit. Lodovico's pride had been soothed by the distinction of having his son live in the palace under the patronage of Lorenzo de' Medici. He was also pleased with the allowance Lorenzo gave the boy, which was turned over to his father. But he was astonished when Michelangelo poured these gold coins into his hand.

"Do you mean to say the Medici paid all this for two pieces of stonecutting!" he exclaimed. He shook his head. "Maybe there is something in this sculpture business after all."

Michelangelo was now in the position of eldest son of the family, for his older brother Lionardo had finished his religious training and had joined the Monastery of Dominican monks, San Marco. Michelangelo accepted the responsibility of helping the family, but sculpture came first and money second. Except for his own necessary expenses whatever he earned would be given to his father.

CHAPTER 4

FRA SAVONAROLA COMES TO FLORENCE

As he lived at the palace among the most distinguished artists, poets and scholars, Michelangelo agreed with them that Florence was the most inspiring city in Italy. It was also a city whose emotional people were absorbed in material pleasures and a liking for pagan thought with its freedom for indulgence.

In Rome a voice of denunciation was raised, that of

48

the fanatical Dominican monk, Fra Savonarola. Soon he came to Florence as prior of the Monastery of San Marco where Michelangelo's brother Lionardo had embraced the religious life. The monk's lean, black-clad figure became a familiar sight in the city as he carried on his campaign for reform.

At first Fra Savonarola was a new sensation and everyone, including artists and scholars, Lorenzo and Michelangelo among them, went to hear him. The monk leaned over the pulpit, fixing his burning eyes on the congregation while he thundered his denunciations and threatened them with the fires of hell for their dissolute life. People trembled, wept, and went into a panic of fear and remorse.

Lorenzo de' Medici did not oppose Savonarola, for intellectually he wanted to hear what the monk had to say. His mood changed, however, as Savonarola accused him and his family, as well as the cardinals and the Pope himself, of evil living. Savonarola declared that Lorenzo de' Medici, in his position as banker and politician, had misused funds of the city to buy pagan art and had led the people away from Christianity into sin. The monk preached against the vices of the Florentines, against their art so closely related to the old paganism the Church had long ago banished from Italy. He preached against the new learning of the scholars and poets. It was a trap that would bring the wrath of God upon them. The

49

Savonarola would rule these people.

people went into prayer and penitence with the same intensity they had given to festivals.

Michelangelo was deeply disturbed. To him, Savonarola seemed like the voice of Dante in *The Divine Comedy*. He felt the truth of the monk's warnings of punishment, for he had seen enough of the voluptuous pursuit of pleasure among the Florentines. He had been worried, as well as tempted, by the pagan freedoms. The accusations against Lorenzo, however, made him indignant. Whatever other members of the family might have done, Lorenzo was, to him, the wise and wonderful leader of the city.

Fra Savonarola was deliberately intending to destroy Lorenzo and the power of the Medicis. He was not only fanatically religious, but a man with a great urge for power. He would rule these people and force them into his ideals of Christian life.

At this time the Florentines were further alarmed by an enemy from outside. News came that Charles VIII, King of France, was invading Italy with an army which was marching toward Florence. Savonarola announced that the French King was the scourge of God, sent to punish the people for their sins, and he prepared to welcome the invader.

In the wild turmoil of fear and emotion that filled Florence, Michelangelo found his world of creative work falling to pieces around him. First the old sculptor, Bertoldo, died, telling Michelangelo that he was the heir of Donatello; he must produce sculpture to honor his city. Then Lorenzo, sick in body and deeply depressed in soul, went for a rest to one of his villas and soon died, in 1492. At the time when another Italian, Christopher Columbus, was discovering a New World, a great era of leadership in the arts died in Florence with Lorenzo the Magnificent.

The two men who had been guide and inspiration to Michelangelo were gone, leaving him completely desolate. He returned to his father's house, although Piero de' Medici, the new head of the family, invited him to stay at the palace. He did not like Piero, and the palace without Lorenzo meant nothing to him. The only commission frivolous Piero offered the sculptor was to carve a snowman in the palace courtyard after an unusually heavy winter snowfall. Grimly Michelangelo did it while the young people of the palace frolicked around him, but he was disgusted. His work would melt away as had the glory of the Medicis.

He must bury himself in the study of sculpture in order to endure his melancholy and loneliness, but what could he do? The Bertoldo studio was disbanded, the antique statues of the garden were overthrown and lying in the grass. There were no commissions and he had no money. Occasionally he visited with Francesco, but the other young artists were dispersed. Art was under a cloud, particularly as some

52

of the artists had become converts to Savonarola's teaching and had renounced their works.

Then Michelangelo remembered his determination to learn more about anatomy by the dissection of bodies. He knew the prior of the charity hospital, Santo Spirito, where destitute people were cared for until they died. Although dissection was against the law in Florence, he took his problem to his friend the prior, who was a man of great understanding. He was permitted to have a key to the morgue where bodies were wrapped in winding sheets before burial, but he must work secretly, in the middle of the night.

Night after night, by candlelight, he labored at this revolting task, urged on by his desire for knowledge. He learned what he needed to know by studying the disposition of muscles, the ingenious way sets of muscles work against one another to maintain the tension and movement of life. The acquisition of knowledge under such circumstances exhausted him, but he was grateful to the prior. In return for the favor he carved a wooden crucifix for the altar of Santo Spirito.

As the French army drew near the city, Savonarola announced he would greet with pleasure the arrival of the French King. In their present mood the people would not fight, that Michelangelo knew. There was no place for him as an artist in Florence. He decided to leave, to find work in some other city.

53

The young sculptor was only seventeen when he left his city in search of freedom to work at his art. He went first to Venice, but that city of dazzling sea and sky had no appeal for him. He journeyed on to the old walled town of Bologna. There he was befriended by one of the leading families, the Aldrovandi, who were friends of the Medici. His patron arranged several commissions for him to carve marble statues for one of the churches. The work was successful, but the favor shown the Florentine roused the jealousy of Bolognese artists. There was trouble again for Michelangelo, as these men were ready to drive him from the city.

After a year in Bologna he had done well and gained some reputation, but he had roused enmity and was lonely. He longed to see his brother and his friend. It was time to go home. With a bag of money and his tools the young sculptor returned to Florence.

CHAPTER 5

MICHELANGELO IN ROME

A young man on horseback rode along the roads of Tuscany, past olive groves and vineyards, past hills crowned with cypresses and villas. On a hilltop the young man drew rein to look down on his home, his dear Florence. It seemed even more beautiful after a year's absence; the tiled-roof houses accented by dark tones of trees, the tower of the campanile and the soaring dome of Il Duomo, the Cathedral. Like a yellow-green ribbon the River Arno wound through the city.

When he came to his father's house his brother Buonarroto welcomed him, and even his father was pleased to see him, particularly since he brought money he had earned in Bologna. It was a lonely home-coming for the artist, with Lorenzo and Bertoldo gone; also his friend Poliziano had died in his absence. He feared that the stimulating companionship in art and thought was no more.

As the home-coming artist wandered through the streets his spirits were yet more depressed. What had happened to this city of vivacious people and constant traffic? What had become of the usual song and laughter in the streets? Under the harsh rule of Fra Savonarola, Florence had become a city of gloom and penance. Charles VIII had entered the city, had demanded a large sum of money to leave Florence alone, and had marched on with his army to Naples. Two cousins of the Medici, Lorenzo and Giovanni, had made peace with the monk and were helping to govern the city. They were living in the Medici palace and had changed their name to Popolano to make the Florentines think they were on the side of the people.

Fra Savonarola had become more extreme in his preaching, more severe in his rule, for he was convinced he represented the voice of God to turn these people from their pagan living. To him, the art and learning developed under Lorenzo de' Medici were part of the sinfulness he had set himself to destroy. He had organized an Army of Boys who invaded homes to carry off works of art, books of the new learning, and items of luxury such as costumes, jewels, cosmetics, all to be burned in the bonfires of "Baubles and Vanities."

Michelangelo learned that his irresponsible younger brothers, Giovansimoni and Sigismondo, had joined the Army of Boys. There was to be a bonfire one evening at the Piazza della Signoria, and the boys defiantly urged Buonarroto and Michelangelo to watch it.

The army of young fanatics, carrying flaming torches, marched through the streets chanting, "Long live Christ, the King of Florence; long live Mary, the Queen." They had gathered bundles of treasures from houses to carry to the Piazza. There the monks of San Marco stood around a huge pyre of wood on which the treasures were heaped. While the flames leaped high the boys and monks chanted. Michelangelo was sick at heart as he watched the hysterical destruction of works of beauty and precious books.

In his distress, next day he went in search of Francesco Granacci and found him at the Ghirlandaio studio. The two friends embraced joyfully.

"Francesco, how do you get along in this sad city?" Michelangelo asked his friend.

Francesco shrugged. "Not too well. Our master

Ghirlandaio died and we are trying to keep the studio together. But what is the use? There is no desire for art or for rich men's portraits in these dark times. And how goes it with you, my friend?"

Michelangelo told him of the commissions Aldrovandi had obtained for him in Bologna.

"I had a good life there and I earned money for my family but, Francesco, I am discouraged. Nothing I have carved in the past year satisfies me. What shall I do now? I have no studio, no marble and no money to buy it."

"I will arrange something for you," said Francesco cheerfully.

In a few days he came to Michelangelo to tell him he had found a chunk of marble and had arranged a place for him to work in the deserted Garden of the Gods.

It was sheer joy to feel the marble under his hands and to try its quality with his tools. Shaping, cutting, polishing, he carved for pleasure a Sleeping Cupid such as the old Roman sculptors had made.

Lorenzo Popolano came into the garden and saw the carving.

"Michelangelo, this Cupid has the style of the old Romans. If you could make it look like an antique, I'll wager I could sell it for you in Rome through a dealer I know. The nobles in that city are enthusiastic over antique sculpture at present."

58

It amused Michelangelo to fool the rich men who knew nothing about art. With no thought beyond trying his skill at aging the marble, he rubbed earth and stain into the smooth new surface. He did not consider the Cupid a serious work.

To his surprise the Roman dealer sold the Sleeping Cupid as an antique piece to Cardinal Riario. He sent Popolano thirty ducats which were turned over to Michelangelo. He did not think it much of a price for a supposedly antique piece of sculpture, but at the moment he was glad of the money for his family.

Before long a messenger arrived from Cardinal Riario to Popolano asking to meet the sculptor of the Sleeping Cupid. The Cardinal had suspected it was a fake, but he wanted the sculptor who could work in such antique style. Leo Baglioni, the messenger, told Michelangelo, "Cardinal Riario paid the dealer two hundred ducats for the piece, but he admires the work so much he doesn't mind the deception."

"Two hundred ducats!" exclaimed Michelangelo. "The dealer sent me only thirty ducats." Then he laughed. "I shouldn't object to being cheated since I fooled the dealer and the Cardinal first."

"Well, come to Rome and try to get from the dealer what he owes you. Cardinal Riario wants you to live in his palace and create sculpture for him."

Here was a chance to leave the city which, for the artist, had become a tragic place. The family needed money as usual. He could work in Rome and send his earnings to them. At the age of twenty-one the young sculptor turned his steps toward Rome, to enter a new phase of creative work.

It was Michelangelo's first glimpse of the Eternal City, once the capital of the Roman Empire and Republic, then the center of Christendom. As he and Baglioni rode through narrow lanes of broken cobblestones with refuse underfoot, past piles of ruins and forlorn shacks between the palaces of the wealthy nobles and cardinals, the young artist was shocked.

Whole districts were abandoned, their buildings sagging in on one another, the rubble piled up in the street. The ancient Roman Forum, center of life under the Republic and Empire, had become a public dump and animal market. From the heaped up rubbish there emerged a few columns, a reminder of the grandeur that had been Rome.

Under the Borgia Pope, Alexander VI, Rome was in a dying condition. The Church, both as a spiritual and temporal power, was approaching a violent crisis. The Pope was warring with powerful families of the city-states and of Rome for control of Rome and central Italy. He intended to enlarge the papal states by seizing cities and was determined to rule like a wealthy secular prince, although he was the spiritual head of the Church.

When Leo Baglioni took Michelangelo to Cardinal

Riario's palace, he was received pleasantly. The Cardinal spoke of his admiration for the Sleeping Cupid and said he wanted the young sculptor to carve a statue for him very soon. Meanwhile Michelangelo was to live in the palace. He was assigned a dark room in the servants' quarters and then, apparently, forgotten. Weeks passed with no word from Cardinal Riario and no work or money. Baglioni warned the young man not to press the Cardinal. He must wait until he was summoned and given permission to carve a statue.

The young sculptor found relief from loneliness and anxiety in the company of numerous Florentines who were living in Rome. From them he gained some comprehension of the intrigues and political schemes that made the city an uneasy, often unsafe, place to live. It was bewildering to the artist and he wanted no part of it, particularly no part in the intrigues of his fellow citizens of Florence. Piero de' Medici, living in exile, was trying to raise troops to attack Florence to win it back from the Medicis who had defected to Savonarola. Presently he marched off with a small company but soon returned, a beaten man, to spend all the family money he could lay hands on. Michelangelo had no sympathy for Piero and his ambition.

He explored the city, marveling at the majestic ruins of ancient Rome, the splendid statuary still in existence, the palaces of the nobility and the cardinals.

He sketched buildings and people.

The dirty streets, the miserable hovels of the poor people, distressed him. He sketched buildings and people, widening his knowledge of humanity through the characters who posed for him. Although he had food and lodging in the palace, he was earning nothing and his attempt to get the money owed him from the dealer who sold the Sleeping Cupid was fruitless.

At last, after many weeks, Cardinal Riario sent for him to discuss the statue he was to carve. While he was making sketches for it, another blow fell. There was an uprising in the Florentine quarter after the Pope excommunicated Savonarola. During the fighting Juan Borgia, a member of the Pope's family, was assassinated. The papal court went into mourning and Cardinal Riario closed his palace, so there was no chance for work. When Michelangelo appealed to his employer, the Cardinal did acknowledge that he should not have kept the young man waiting so long. As a recompense he gave him the block of marble that had been bought. Now he had marble, but no studio and no employer.

Good fortune favored him when he met the Roman banker, Jacopo Galli, who was a friend of the Cardinal and of some Florentines. This man had seen a cartoon that Michelangelo drew for the Cardinal's barber and was pleased with it. He wanted to meet the artist. Michelangelo told Jacopo Galli about his fruitless year waiting to work for the Cardinal, and that he was left with only a block of marble.

"Well, my young friend, suppose you create sculpture for me," Jacopo Galli proposed. "I would like you to carve me a life-sized statue of Bacchus, the ancient god of wine, for my garden. Move the marble to my garden and live with me while you work. I will pay you three hundred ducats."

Happy to be at work, Michelangelo threw himself into the task with concentrated energy after the long months of waiting. The chips flew as the tools cut into the block, while Michelangelo strove to bring forth his conception of the Greek god of wine. He knew the story of Bacchus well from conversations with Poliziano at the Medici palace.

His Bacchus was a beautiful figure of a young man with the physical perfection of the Greeks and the self-indulgence of a young Roman of the Renaissance. Bacchus holds a cup of wine; he sways slightly; his lips are parted and his eyes glazed. Behind him crouches a goat-legged satyr holding up a bunch of grapes.

Michelangelo's conception was not entirely that of the Greeks—the young god celebrating the purple wine. Quite evidently the wine, not the god, is in control in Michelangelo's Bacchus. He had expressed his belief that man's life was more than pleasure and physical perfection; he was a spiritual being as well. He must master nature or be mastered.

When artists and intellectuals gathered in Galli's

64

garden to admire the exquisite statue, they noticed the difference from the Greek conception. This sculptor had expressed the Renaissance reverence for the ancient past, but had added his own rejection of pagan ideals.

All the artists gave high praise to the beautiful Bacchus. It was a marvelous work of sculpture from any point of view, but especially remarkable because of the youthfulness of the sculptor. The fame of the new young sculptor spread through the city. Michelangelo knew a time of exaltation over his success.

CHAPTER **6**

THE PIETÀ FOR ST. PETER'S

While Michelangelo was enjoying his success and the praise of the artists, his brother Buonarroto came to visit him. He was overawed by his brother's fame.

"Is Father pleased?" Michelangelo asked.

"Yes, he is, but he thinks that now you are famous you can send him money to get out of debt. He has made another bad investment that failed, so now he has no money. The young brothers are no good and I have only a poor position."

"But I sent him almost all the money I made for carving the Bacchus," the sculptor exclaimed.

"I know, but he spent it badly."

"I don't want to borrow money from a banker I know, but it may be that I shall get another commission soon, Buonarroto," he said anxiously.

Buonarroto told him not to worry and went on to relate news of the family and of Florence. Most important, he gave Michelangelo a first-hand account of what had happened after the Pope excommunicated Savonarola.

"Do you know, the monk dared to defy the Pope after he had been excommunicated," he said. "The people were shocked and a little frightened, too. We were all weary of Fra Savonarola's severity, and the city council was afraid the Pope would cut off trade because of the monk's acts. They appointed a committee that arrested Savonarola and his two aides, Fra Domenico and Fra Silvestre. Then the monks were tried and Fra Savonarola was tortured, my brother, to make him confess he was not inspired by God. He refused, of course, so he was declared a heretic, along with his companions, and condemned to death!"

"*Dio mio*," exclaimed Michelangelo. "Savonarola was a man of God, after all."

"Yes, my brother, and I can tell you the execution was a dreadful sight, one I shall never forget. Gibbets were put up in the Piazza della Signoria. Savonarola and the other two monks were hung, then fires were lighted under the gibbets and the bodies were burned. Afterward the ashes were thrown into the Arno."

Michelangelo was horrified. "Oh, my poor Florentines," he cried, "how could you be so sacrilegious. Fra Savonarola was a man who believed he was doing God's will, and he stood by his convictions even unto a martyr's death."

This news from Florence depressed him after his brother departed. Fortunately, a new commission came to distract him from his sadness. Jacopo Galli told him that the saintly old French Cardinal, Jean de la Groslaye, had seen the Bacchus, that he was deeply impressed with its beauty, with the vitality and perfection of the carving.

"The Cardinal wants you to create a large sculpture for him, to stand in the Chapel of the French Kings in St. Peter's. He has the Pope's permission to do this."

"A sculpture of mine to stand in St. Peter's," said Michelangelo, awe-struck. "God is good to me."

It was Jacopo Galli who steered his young protegé through the negotiations for the contract. Galli wrote one of the most remarkable art contracts ever drawn up. The banker, on behalf of Michelangelo and with his own fortune as security, guaranteed that the new marble statue "shall be more beautiful than any work of marble to be seen in Rome" and, further, that no living sculptor would be able to do as well. The statue was to be completed within a year.

The commission was a challenge to Michelangelo's deep creative strength, never yet fully used, and it required all his skill, but the young sculptor was confident and full of joy. First of all he went to St. Peter's to look at the Chapel of the French Kings. The ancient basilica, the most important church in the Christian world, was in a dilapidated condition and looked neglected. He studied the niche where the statue would stand in the chapel. It was rather deep, but he would consider that when he designed the marble.

Cardinal Groslaye was delighted with Michelangelo's choice of subject—the Pietà, or Sorrow, a popular subject with many sculptors and painters. It represents the moment after the Crucifixion when Christ is taken from the cross and given to his mother while other figures, generally Mary Magdalene and St. John, stand beside her. There was a technical reason for this composition. The horizontal body of the dead Christ is much longer than the seated figure of the Virgin. If the vertical figures are added, the composition is improved. Michelangelo had a different conception. He desired to portray only the grieving Mother with her dead Son across her lap.

69

While he was thinking, dreaming and making sketches, his brother visited him once more. He found that the young sculptor had moved from Jacopo Galli's house to a poor, bare room and was not eating enough. Together the brothers searched for and found a place with a large room for studio and a smaller room with a fireplace for cooking. They bargained with a dealer for the simple necessities of furniture and moved them in, along with the sculptor's workbench, tools, and block of marble. Michelangelo was delighted with the place, but to Buonarroto it looked stark and uncomfortable.

"Take care of yourself, Michelagnolo," he said, using the family nickname. "Try to remember to eat enough. And don't worry about Father's complaints. We are getting along well enough, and I shall tell him you have a splendid commission from a Cardinal." The brothers embraced and Buonarroto returned to Florence.

The sculptor strewed his workshop with discarded drawings, as he struggled to give perfect form to his vision of the Mother and the Christ. In his imagination he saw the Virgin as a youthful woman, a memory of his own mother so long dead. He did not wish to portray her as a mature woman worn with grief, the usual conception. As he explained to Cardinal Groslaye, the Virgin was always pure, therefore she would not age.

70

Michelangelo put his whole strength into the Pietà.

He also had the technical problem of the relation of size: how a slender woman could hold a grown man across her lap. This he solved by modeling the Virgin on a slightly larger scale than the figure of her Son. The illusion of size was increased by the heavy draperies—the head covering of the Virgin, the voluminous folds of her garments at the sides and around her feet. For months Michelangelo worked from dawn to dark, bringing out from the marble the perfect figures. Winter came and his room was so cold that his fingers were stiff and he tried to carve with mittened hands.

In the spring Cardinal Groslaye came to the workshop to see how his Pietà was advancing. He was greatly pleased with the work, but begged the sculptor to hurry towards completion. The Cardinal was old and sick. He felt he had not long to live, and the greatest desire of his heart was to see the Pietà installed in the chapel and to dedicate it before he died.

Michelangelo understood that wish; he put his whole strength into the effort to finish the statue by laboring not only all day but through the night. He tried to work by the light of a small lamp, but it was too dim. Then he made a hat of stiff, folded paper with a wire around it and a loop to hold a candle in front. With his head bent close to the marble, the candle gave enough light by which to chisel and

72

carve. The melted wax dripped down over his eyebrows, but he ignored it. He forgot food, forgot to rest or sleep as he worked in a fury of creation.

The Cardinal did not live to dedicate his Pietà. He died while there were still some months of work required to complete the statue. Michelangelo consulted Jacopo Galli about what he should do. The sculpture was designed for the niche in the Chapel of the French Kings, but did he have the right to place it there now the Cardinal was dead? Galli told him to go ahead, they would find a way to take it to St. Peter's. "You have fulfilled the contract, my friend," said the banker. "This is the most beautiful marble sculpture the Romans have ever seen."

When the statue was finished, Michelangelo engaged some of the strong-armed workers from the stone yard, who were his friends, to help him move it. With infinite labor the men carried the heavy piece of sculpture to a wagon and slowly drove it to St. Peter's. It took all their strength to remove it from the wagon, carry it up the steps, and to its place in the chapel. When it was established the men, sweating and exhausted, knelt and prayed before the exquisite vision of the Mother and Son.

The glorious Pietà rested in the place it was to occupy for centuries, gazed upon with wonder and reverence by thousands of people. The lovely face

73

of the Mother is bent over her dead Son, his head supported by one arm, his limp body cradled across her lap. She gazes down at Him with tenderness, compassion and resigned sorrow, a symbol of all grieving mothers who have accepted God's will. In these wonderful figures Michelangelo expressed his deep faith in the harmony of God and humanity. For most Christians since then Michelangelo's vision of the grieving Mother and her dead Son has been the image of this tragic moment in the story of Jesus.

In 1964 the people of our country may have the opportunity to study this masterpiece for themselves. Pope John XXIII has agreed to send the precious sculpture to stand in the Vatican pavilion at the 1964 World's Fair in New York.

Every day after the Pietà was installed, Michelangelo went to St. Peter's to look at it, to hear what people said about it as they stopped to wonder and admire. They did not know where it came from or who created it, but they were moved by its beauty and meaning. One day he heard visitors from Lombardy declare the sculpture was made by one of their artists known as "the hunchback of Milan."

That evening Michelangelo was back in the dark church, hammer and chisel in hand, a candle to light his way. The Virgin of the Pietà has a band across the breast and over one shoulder. Upon this band the sculptor carved in traditional Latin form, "Michel-

74

angelo of Florence Made This." It was the only time he set a signature to his work.

Rome had nothing more for the young sculptor at that time. He longed for Florence, for the artistic vitality of its people which was surely reviving now that the stern monk, Fra Savonarola, was no more. The lonely young man wanted the companionship of family and friends. Quietly he gathered up his tools and a few possessions, rented a mule, and set out for Florence.

CHAPTER 7

THE GIANT DAVID

The faithful friend, Francesco Granacci, welcomed Michelangelo to his home town in the spring
of 1501 with a hearty embrace.

"*Caro mio*, we are all so proud of you—the best
sculptor in all Italy—and you are ours, you belong to
Florence."

Francesco took him at once to a club of artists who
had returned to Florence after the death of Fra Savonarola. Now they could paint or carve as they liked,

and they were full of enthusiasm. Michelangelo discovered that the fame of his Bacchus and the Pietà had preceded him. It was a satisfaction to know that he was now a person of importance among artists and politicians. The artists organized a gay, sumptuous dinner to celebrate his fame, and he was made a member of the group.

At home his heart was warmed by his father's respect and affection. Lodovico was at last convinced that his son was a success even though it was in sculpture, since he had produced great works for a cardinal and a banker in Rome and had been well paid. The old man began making plans for this successful son to help the family.

"You must open a studio, Michelangelo," he said. "You will have all the commissions you can handle. You can set up a wool shop for Buonarroto and find a job for Giovansimoni. Sigismondo is only earning a few scudi as a professional soldier."

"Yes, Father, I must have a place to work," Michelangelo said patiently. "There are great opportunities here. I have plans you will hear about later."

It was a joy to wander through the streets of the revived city and to spend hours with artist friends after those lonely, hard-working years in Rome. It was a good time for artists to obtain commissions for portraits, altar paintings or sculpture, since Florence was once more prosperous, its people vividly alive;

77

traders were busy, politicians were working to advance the restored Republic of Florence. It was governed once more by officers of the Signoria, headed by an honest, respected citizen, Piero Soderini, the gonfalonier or president.

The people had recovered from the penitential gloom imposed by Savonarola and from the hysterical reaction against him which led to his execution. Florentines were ashamed of that uncivilized act and were ready to admit that Savonarola had been sincere and had done some good for the city. To this day neither the city nor the universal Church has made up its mind about the impassioned monk. There are always Catholics ready to venerate him as a saint despite the Pope's condemnation.

In this happy place Michelangelo's creative energy flourished. Almost immediately a letter from Jacopo Galli brought him a commission to carve fifteen small statues of saints for Cardinal Piccolomini, to stand on an altar in Siena. The pay would be five hundred ducats, and he was expected to finish the statues in three years. Michelangelo was not interested in carving these figures, but he could not refuse and signed the contract in June, 1501. By August the sculptor had signed another contract which would require three years.

He was commissioned by the city council and the

Cathedral officers to create a colossal statue, to honor the Florentine Republic, from a huge block of marble in their possession. Ever since he had returned home, the sculptor had been obsessed by the desire to carve a statue from that tremendous block which had been lying in the Cathedral work yard for forty years. It had originally been intended for a statue of Hercules to ornament one of the pillars of Brunelleschi's great dome on Il Duomo. The stone had been damaged in transportation from the quarry, and an old-time sculptor had further injured it by chiseling it badly, after which he abandoned it. No other sculptor had been willing to touch it.

Day after day Michelangelo went to the Cathedral yard to gaze upon the towering block of marble, over fourteen feet high. The block was too tall, too thin in the middle for its height, in the opinion of many sculptors. Any figure carved from it would be a giant, twice life size, but that was just what Michelangelo wanted. His work in Rome had given him confidence in his skill, and the Pietà in particular had been such a deeply spiritual and emotional creation that he longed to work on a gigantic scale.

A giant was also just what the Signoria wanted, to be the symbol of their republican city. The commission had been offered to Leonardo da Vinci. That great painter, engineer and inventor was never devoted to sculpture, however, and he was about to enter a spell of service with Cesare Borgia who was a military adventurer. He wanted Leonardo's talents given to the design of engines of war. Leonardo had refused the commission because, as he said, sculpture was an art inferior to painting; it was too mechanical, too much the work of stonecutters. When this remark reached the ears of Michelangelo he resented it angrily, and he also thought it was traitorous of Leonardo to work for Cesare Borgia who would without doubt try, eventually, to conquer Florence. The scornful remark about sculpture added to the antagonism Michelangelo felt toward this man, older than himself and a Florentine, who was hailed as the foremost artist in Italy. It may be that this resentment increased his urge to carve a giant, to show Leonardo that a masterpiece of sculpture could be created.

On August 16, 1501, the city officials announced that worthy Master Michelangelo Buonarroti had been given the commission to carve a giant statue from the block. They had decided to keep their famous sculptor at home; otherwise he would go to Siena to finish the commission for Cardinal Piccolomini. They advised him to postpone work on that contract.

The sculptor had carved a few of the statues for the Cardinal, but the contract was never completed, and that failure disturbed him for years. The huge block of marble and the trust of the city of Florence were too great a temptation.

When Michelangelo told his father about the Signoria contract, Lodovico reacted as usual with financial questions.

"What will the Signoria pay you, son, and how long will it take to finish the work?"

"Two years, Father, and the city will pay me six florins a month."

"So! That adds up to only a hundred and forty-four florins. The Piccolomini contract will pay more than twice that sum. You should keep on with that work."

"The city will pay me more when the statue is finished if they are pleased. And I cannot do otherwise; I shall carve this statue for Florence."

His father's criticism was offset by the unselfish joy of his fellow artists, who celebrated his success with a gay evening of food and drink.

"Long live Michelangelo!" shouted Francesco. "Success to the best sculptor in Italy!"

Michelangelo concentrated all thought and feeling on the choice of a heroic figure to symbolize Republican Florence. He studied the Old Testament heroes and an inspiration came to him. He would carve David, the shepherd boy, who with a stone from a sling killed the Philistines' giant Goliath, thus turning

81

the tide of battle to save the people of Israel from a dangerous enemy. Even so the Republic of Florence, surrounded by princely and imperial enemies, mustered its strength to maintain its freedom.

For days Michelangelo studied the huge block, measuring, figuring out how the strong young man of his imagination could be chiseled out of the unwieldy shape of the marble block. He made countless sketches and modeled figures in wax.

How should he portray David? In the moment of triumph after slaying Goliath? Instead, Michelangelo modeled the vigorous youth poised for action, with the sling over the left shoulder, just before the throw. The expression on the wonderfully carved face when it was completed was one of determination and deep thought. At that moment David was emerging as the hero of Israel to serve God and his people.

Now he was face to face with his giant. Michelangelo engaged artisans in the Cathedral yard to move the great block on rollers, with block and tackle, to a corner of the yard that would be his. The men built a crude wooden shed around the marble and constructed scaffolding within so the sculptor could work at any angle. Michelangelo made a key to the shed and allowed no one to enter. His tools attacked the marble keenly, feeling out the shape within. For days and for months he worked, while the chips flew and marble dust coated his hair and clothes and

The stately head rose above the crate.

clogged his nostrils. He felt that divine help was giving him the energy to carry on this intensity of creative work. Often he flung himself to the ground in his clothes to take a few hours rest, grudging the extra time needed to go to his house.

Sometimes, when he did not come home at dark, Buonarroto came to the shed, bringing supper. Once Francesco Granacci came and knocked on the door, hearing the frenzy of tools cutting marble within.

"Come out, Michelangelo," he shouted. "You will kill yourself with work. Come and spend a merry evening with your fellow artists—it will do you good."

"No, no, go away, Francesco," was the irritated reply from the shed. "I have to work."

After some months Piero Soderini came with members of the council to view progress, and they were well pleased. Their David was emerging from the marble. They stipulated that the statue must be completed within two years, then presented the sculptor with four hundred florins, which were welcome in the Buonarroti home.

Time went on and the sculptor was often distracted by other affairs, but continued his intensive labors on the David. As he worked on the splendid head he thought constantly of the spirit of his beloved city and also remembered the spirit of the great Florentine, Lorenzo de' Medici, his friend, who had led his city to its most glorious period of culture and art. His David must symbolize both.

84

At last, in the autumn of 1503, the giant David was completed, perfected and polished to the sculptor's satisfaction. A committee of Florentines, including Leonardo da Vinci and Botticelli, met to appraise it and to determine its location. They all acknowledged that Michelangelo had created a masterpiece. It could not be placed on top of the Cathedral where it would never be seen. They decided, with Michelangelo's consent, that the David should stand beside the main entrance to the Palace of the Signoria.

The moving of the huge statue was a triumph of ingenuity. One wall of the shed was knocked out and the marble was raised on heavy wooden rollers, then it was enclosed in a wooden frame and lashed into position with ropes. Forty men dragged the great crate through the streets, slowly, slowly, while crowds gathered to watch. The stately head rose above the crate almost on the level with roofs of houses. It took four days to cover the few blocks to its location. Another three weeks passed before the statue was released from the crate and placed in position.

Florentines came day after day to gaze with wonder at their giant that stood in strength and beauty, in the shining purity of white marble, before their seat of government.

"This statue is our city, this is our spirit of freedom," was the comment that came from all people— from workers to artists and politicians. In the giant

85

David, Florentines saw themselves, holding off the mighty political forces ranged against them. The people always called the statue "The Giant."

In 1504, at the age of twenty-nine, Michelangelo had contributed two of the fundamental images that mankind has since carried about in their heads as part of the common language of humanity. He was a hero in his home town and in all artistic Italy. The sculptor himself had much of the spirit he carved into the face and body of David—the hero passing from private contemplation to public and large-scale action.

CHAPTER 8

THE CONTEST WITH
LEONARDO DA VINCI

The carving of the giant David was more than
enough to keep one artist completely occupied, but
Michelangelo managed to do other work in the same
period of several years. He felt so sure of himself after
his successes that he was ready to undertake any project that was offered.

From this time on he would often pray, as he
dreamed of great works in marble, "Lord, grant that

87

I shall always want to do more than I can." That expressed the spirit of this great genius as, in his later life, he plunged into tremendous undertakings.

Piero Soderini, the gonfalonier of the Signoria, asked the sculptor to carve the Twelve Apostles in marble for Il Duomo. The Signoria would make him the official sculptor of Florence, and the contract would include a house and studio. Michelangelo knew this meant years of work, but he could not resist the opportunity.

While work began on the new house, he set up a block of marble in his studio and began to carve a statue of St. Matthew for Il Duomo. Then he was distracted by a request from a man he had known as a boy, Agnolo Doni. He had become a wealthy merchant in the wool business and was engaged to marry a daughter of the aristocratic Strozzi family. He wanted Michelangelo to paint a circular picture, called a tondo, as a wedding present for his bride, the subject to be the Holy Family.

The sculptor did not think much of painting in oils or tempera, but he was in a mood to demonstrate that he could create art in any medium. The sharp bargaining of his merchant friend over the price almost made him refuse to paint the picture, but a price of sixty florins was finally agreed upon.

Michelangelo proceeded to paint the group of the Holy Family within the circular form of the tondo.

His Madonna was a healthy, happy young woman, turning as she holds the Child on her shoulder, while St. Joseph bends over the two in voluminous robes. The eye is carried upward by the folds of the Madonna's garments, the twist of her torso, her raised arms and eyes. This pyramidal composition stabilizes the circle. The composition is further held upright by a line of wall in the background, with figures of athletes standing or leaning against it.

When Agnolo Doni saw the picture he was furious. "What is there holy about this picture?" he shouted. "You have painted the Madonna like a peasant woman, and what are those nude figures doing in the background? You must do it over."

"If you don't like it, you need not take it," replied the artist, "but I do not release you from your contract. And if you do take it, the price will be not sixty florins, but one hundred and forty."

The merchant shouted with rage and went off in a huff. However, he had boasted all over town that the great Michelangelo was painting a Holy Family as a wedding gift to his bride, and he would be a laughing stock if he did not have it.

Soon he returned, threw a bag of gold coins on the artist's table, and carried off the picture. Florentines had followed this bargaining episode eagerly, and everyone laughed when the sculptor outwitted the penny-pinching merchant. Michelangelo did not reckon his work in money terms, but he took this opportunity to demonstrate to the commercial-minded merchant that an artist could not be beaten down and cheapened on prices like an ordinary tradesman or artisan, and he thoroughly enjoyed the episode. This picture has been called the Doni Madonna.

During this same period Michelangelo also carved a Madonna and Child for a group of Flemish merchants who sent it to their home in Bruges, now Belgium. It announced to the northland that a mighty sculptor had arisen in the South. It was at this time, too, that Michelangelo took up the study of poetry and began to write sonnets himself.

The real challenge to Michelangelo's genius after the David was the plan of the Signoria for the glorification of Florence by frescoes in the Great Hall of the Council. Like every city-state in Italy, the Republic had a long military history. To preserve its independence and extend its dominions, the state had taken on and bested most of the city-states of central and northern Italy, and had also fought off the forces of France and the Holy Roman Empire of Germany and Austria. One wall of the Council Hall was to be decorated; half was offered to Leonardo da Vinci, and Michelangelo obtained the contract for the other half.

Leonardo da Vinci had been living for a long time in Milan, creating his masterpieces of drawing and painting under the patronage of the Duke of Milan. When the Duke died in 1504, Leonardo returned to his native Florence. Piero Soderini and the Signoria were eager to have the Master paint the fresco in the Council Hall and offered him a generous fee. Michelangelo had not painted frescoes, although he learned the technique while a student in Ghirlandaio's studio. He wanted the rivalry with the older and more famous artist, whose work he admired, although he could not feel friendly to him as a personality.

The two men of genius, Leonardo and Michelangelo, were so utterly different in temperament and ideas that they could not appreciate each other. It must be admitted that most of the antagonism and all of the rudeness that occurred when the two clashed were the fault of Michelangelo. Leonardo was coolly aloof, with a keenly scientific mind, a gracious, dignified figure, every inch the master. His beard and long reddish hair flowed over the lace at the neck of his robes, which were always of rich colors and fabrics. His white, beautiful hands did not seem to Michelangelo the hands of an artist; they were a contrast to his own bony, work-worn ones. Michelangelo never cared for good clothes. He went about in dark, simple doublet and cloak and wore high boots. His stocky figure with a big head of curly hair, small forked beard, the flat nose and piercing eyes under frowning brows, was a sharp contrast to Leonardo's elegance.

Now the two men were in keen rivalry over the frescoes in the Council Hall. The Florentines were excited over this contest between their two great artists, and bets were laid on which would create the best fresco.

Despite Leonardo's reputation for superb draughtsmanship, Michelangelo had full confidence that his drawing would equal, if not surpass, that of Leonardo. In 1504 the work began, each artist working on hundreds of sketches and the huge cartoon in his own studio.

The students and artists of Florence and many from other cities came to watch the progress of the cartoons in each artist's studio. Among them was the charming young painter of Urbino, Raphael Sanzio, destined to become the third in the great Renaissance trinity of artists. Already at the age of twenty-one he had a reputation for the compelling sweetness of his painting, but after watching these two masters his work took on a strengthening of figures and compositions. Raphael was always ready to acknowledge his debt to Michelangelo.

As the two master artists filled their huge cartoons with magnificently drawn figures in dramatic compositions, they found themselves the creators of a new school of art for the numerous students and artists who watched them. The cartoons formed the style and thought of artists in Italy for generations.

The two artists, in choice of subject, followed the

92

desire of the Signoria to have the frescoes commemorate the historic military glory of the Republic of Florence.

The subject of Leonardo's fresco was the Battle of Anghiara in which the Florentines defeated the Milanese. Leonardo was devoted to horses; he had made serious studies of their anatomy and had painted and drawn them countless times. He had even tried a heroic statue of horse and rider which had not been finished. His cartoon, therefore, pictured a frenzied swarm of splendid war horses and armored riders struggling to win the battle flag of the enemy. Faces were contorted in fear, hatred, or triumph. The cartoon promised a painting that would be an encyclopedia of human emotions.

Leonardo chose a composition that enabled him to use horses, while Michelangelo, who was absorbed in expressing humanity through the actions and emotions of human bodies, built his composition around them. His subject was the Battle of Cascina, in one of the frequent wars between Florence and their subject city of Pisa. Michelangelo chose a moment in the conflict when the Florentine troops, thinking themselves safe, had stripped to bathe and refresh themselves in a stream. As they bathed, the enemy attacked. The men struggled to get out of the water and into their armor, in a composition that was a frantic swirl of naked or half-clothed soldiers. His cartoon promised a painting that would be an encyclopedia of the hu-

93

The rivalry between the two geniuses ended.

man body in action. His absorption in this is shown
by the fact that he did not call his cartoon a battle;
he named it The Bathers.

Leonardo began to paint his fresco before Michelangelo had finished his cartoon. This great artist was always experimenting with new techniques in painting, and he liked to make changes and repaint as he went along, putting in finishing touches as he thought of them. This could not be done in true fresco, for changes cannot be made after the colors are painted on the wet plaster without cutting out the plaster and starting over again. For this reason Leonardo experimented with other media. By using experimental materials he had ruined his own masterpiece, The Last Supper. Even in his lifetime the paint was already flaking off and becoming dim. Nevertheless, the masterpiece has survived in the mind of man through copies and through repainting by other artists.

Leonardo da Vinci started experimenting with his painting in the Council Hall. No one is certain just what he was trying to do. One theory is that he was using a medium with his oil paint that kept it from drying. Others believe he was trying the ancient method called encaustic painting, using colors mixed with wax which must be kept warm in order to have the wax fuse with the paint.

To keep the wax at the right temperature Leonardo had built fires on the floor near the wall. He had tried this method before in a small hall with success, but the walls in the Council Hall were high and the artist piled on more fuel to send heat up the wall, with disastrous effect. He had already completed a group of warriors on horseback in richly glowing colors, according to those who saw it. But as the heat became greater the wax mixed with the paint began to melt. To the horror of the spectators, all the rich color, the picture of fighting men and rearing horses, ran down the wall and ended in a vast smear on the wall and floor.

Michelangelo forgot his resentment toward Leonardo in his distress for a fellow artist whose year of work had been ruined. He hurried to Leonardo's house.

"Messer Leonardo," he said, "I come to apologize for my rudeness to you in the past, and to express my sorrow that your great fresco is lost."

Courteously Leonardo replied, "I, too, should apologize for my remarks about sculpture that hurt you. I thank you for your concern, and I am sure your fresco of the Battle of Cascina will be a glory to Florence."

The rivalry between two men of genius ended in reconciliation, but the work of their contest was lost to the world. Michelangelo finished his cartoon, but never painted the fresco. Both cartoons were cherished by the city of Florence and studied by many artists until they were lost or destroyed in tempestuous times to come.

In choosing Michelangelo and Leonardo da Vinci, Piero Soderini had certainly picked the best, but he had also chosen two extremely unreliable artists. Both undertook to do more than they could hope to fulfill. Both were subject to the imperious demands of other patrons and the demands of their own growing and shifting interests.

A new challenge was presented to Michelangelo by another patron, the most formidable in Italy, Pope Julius II.

Rapid changes had been taking place while Michelangelo was in Florence. Pope Alexander VI had died. He was succeeded by Pius III, the Cardinal Piccolomini for whom Michelangelo had done five out of fifteen pieces of altar statuary. The sculptor feared he would be ordered to complete that contract, but Pius III lived but a few months. He was succeeded by Cardinal della Rovere of an important Roman family who became Pope Julius II, one of the most brilliant of the Renaissance Popes.

The new pontiff was a man of vigorous body and mind. He was a diplomat, an able soldier, and he intended to strengthen the papal states. The Church, as temporal ruler of central Italy and of various other states throughout Europe and as spiritual ruler of Christendom, was being challenged by great states of Europe and their allies in Italy.

Pope Julius also planned ambitiously to restore Rome to its proper position as the spiritual capital of the world. He would rebuild the city and make it glorious with works of art and architecture. At the time of the High Renaissance, Italy was blessed with splendid artists. Their work would make this period a time that men have looked upon with awe ever since. Pope Julius had work for them all. He sent for architects, sculptors, and painters to glorify Rome.

In the midst of his absorption with the cartoon for the fresco in the Council Hall and the carving of the St. Matthew for Il Duomo, Michelangelo received a summons from Pope Julius to come to Rome; there was work for him. The sculptor did not want to go, for there was so much unfinished work to be done in Florence. When he consulted Piero Soderini, the gonfalonier said, "A Pope's summons cannot be refused; you must go. We will hold your contracts for you until you return."

Once more Michelangelo changed his life and work, this man who always "wanted to do more than he could." He left behind a record of unfinished work that was to grow as time went on. He had never completed the statues for Cardinal Piccolomini; he had not painted his fresco in the Council Hall; he had started only one of the statues in his contract for the Twelve Apostles for Il Duomo. These uncompleted works troubled his conscience throughout his life.

After he had said farewell to his family and friends, Michelangelo mounted his horse and set out for Rome. This was in 1505. He was entering on a new and heroic phase of his life.

CHAPTER 9

POPE JULIUS II AND MICHELANGELO

When Michelangelo rode through the streets of Rome he saw on every hand the changes that were taking place under the new Pope. Streets had been cleared and widened, sagging houses had been torn down and new buildings erected in their place.

He found his Florentine architect friend, Giuliano da San Gallo, who had been appointed official architect of Rome. He was living in one of Pope Julius' palaces and had a large workroom where young apprentices were drawing up plans under his direction for rebuilding the city.

San Gallo took his sculptor friend to meet his patron and learn what his orders were. The Pope was sitting on a great throne surrounded by courtiers and attendants. Julius II, although sixty-two years of age, was a big, powerful man of compelling personality. His gray beard jutted out over the high collar of his robes as he leaned forward to greet the two men, and one hand grasped a stick. The impatient tapping of that stick expressed the tempestuous character of the Holy Father. Courtiers and attendants reacted quickly to that tapping, either hurrying to receive the Pope's commands or sliding out of the way if he was angry.

San Gallo and Michelangelo knelt to kiss the papal ring. When they rose, the imperious eyes of the Pope bored into the equally proud eyes of the sculptor. The two men faced each other and recognized their likeness—two bold, forceful characters of great ideas and soaring imagination.

"Michelangelo de Buonarroti," said Pope Julius, "I have chosen you to carve my tomb. I have seen your Pietà in St. Peter's and I know you are the sculptor I want. My tomb shall also stand in St. Peter's. It shall be a tomb such as the world has not seen since the days of the Roman Emperors."

Michelangelo said quietly, "Yes, Your Holiness, and will you be so kind as to tell me your plans?"

Pope Julius launched into an enthusiastic description of the tomb he was planning. It should be free-standing, not against a wall, and should be an architectural creation ornamented with colossal statues. It should have three levels, with statues on each, and a frieze of bronze figures. The tomb would announce that its occupant, Pope Julius himself, had been of supreme importance to the Church.

Despite the fact that he was somewhat staggered by the order to create a tomb for a celebrity who was still vigorously alive, Michelangelo's imagination took fire from the Pope's description of his plans. A studio was arranged for him near the Vatican palace. There the sculptor went happily to work, measuring, figuring, composing the design of the monumental tomb. Frequently the Pope visited him to talk over the characters to be portrayed in statues: Moses, the law-giver, should occupy one corner of the first level, and the Apostle Paul the opposite corner. As they discussed plans for other figures, the two men of tremendous ideas became friends. They had not yet clashed.

Pope Julius told his sculptor to visit the marble quarries of Carrara to choose the mass of marble that would be needed. He was to leave at once and would be provided with one thousand ducats to pay for the stones.

"Yes, Your Holiness, and what will be paid for the sculpturing?"

"When the tomb is finished you will be paid ten thousand ducats," said his formidable patron haughtily.

Michelangelo's heart sank. It was a very small price for years of work, and it would not be paid until the tomb was complete. Yet he must carve those marbles, and he trusted his patron to help with money when needed. Once more the sculptor who always "wanted to do more than he could" undertook the execution of a dream that could never be fulfilled.

Before he left the city for the Carrara quarries, Michelangelo went with his friend San Gallo to St. Peter's to see where the tomb could be placed. They decided there was no room in the ancient basilica for such a tremendous tomb. San Gallo suggested that a chapel could be built adjacent to the basilica designed to fit the tomb. He would like to design that chapel. He told Michelangelo that the Pope had in mind the restoration of the ancient church. Another architect, Bramante, the chief architect of Italy, had become high in favor with Pope Julius. He and San Gallo were to submit plans for the restoration. Michelangelo was excited over this scheme.

He left for the mountains in high spirits, on horseback with two servants. Eight happy months were spent among the glistening cliffs of the Carrara mountains. The stonecutters of the quarry liked him because he knew so much about marble, and he personally chose the stones that should be cut for the great blocks he needed. As he looked at the gleaming white cliffs of marble he had a fantastic dream of someday carving a colossal figure on the face of the mountain. Finally the great blocks were assembled at a seaport and carried by ship up the Tiber River to Rome. When they were spread out in the meadows behind Michelangelo's house, people came to wonder at the mass of marble blocks.

While he was engrossed in this part of the operation, Michelangelo was distracted by the discovery of an ancient sculpture that had been bricked up in a wall of the baths of Titus. With his friend San Gallo, the sculptor hurried to the scene, eager to see the figure brought to light for the first time in centuries. It was recognized by artists from the description by the Latin writer, Livy. It was the Laocoon, one of the fabled masterpieces of antiquity. For generations sculptors had tried to imagine the work. Here it was before them. The sight instantly set Michelangelo to conceiving new forms for his work.

Laocoon was the Trojan priest who, when Odysseus left the great wooden horse on the beach, cried out, "Beware of the Greeks bearing gifts." He struck the horse with his spear and the sound was hollow, for the wooden horse was filled with Odysseus' troops. The gods, who sided with Odysseus, sent sea serpents to the beach to destroy Laocoon. The sculpture represented the mighty struggle of Laocoon and his sons to escape from the coils of the sea serpents. It was a work of intense emotion, fear and power that appealed greatly to Michelangelo.

He had a struggle of his own coming up, for he found himself in trouble immediately. The thousand ducats had paid for the stones but no more. He had to pay the workers who unloaded the blocks; he needed money for living expenses and to pay the stonecutter assistants he would need in his work. It was necessary to borrow money for the dock workers from a banker he knew. He was eager to get to work; he must see the Pope to ask for financial help, but the Pope was inaccessible.

Michelangelo learned from San Gallo what had been happening during his absence. The great architect, Bramante, an ambitious, unscrupulous man, had won first place with Pope Julius. San Gallo himself had been demoted to second place. The Pope had already decided to build a new choir in St. Peter's to house his tomb. Then Bramante proposed a daring plan, one that suited the Pope and the ambitious architect as well. Why not tear down the old St. Peter's entirely; why not build a new church, a new St.

104

Peter's surpassing all other buildings in grandeur—a fit temple for the head of the Christian Church? Pope Julius was enthusiastic and became absorbed in the plans for St. Peter's.

Michelangelo was never a courtier, a man able to flatter and use pleasant talk to work his way with princes. He tried to go directly to the Pope to ask for the assistance he needed and to discuss the statues for the tomb. He found it difficult to get an audience, but finally presented himself to Julius.

The Holy Father was surrounded with courtiers; he was busy with various subjects, and at the moment was quarreling with a jeweler about prices. Michelangelo heard him say that he did not intend to spend a farthing more on stones, big or little. The Pope greeted his sculptor in an offhand way, paying no attention to his report about the arrival of the marble or his need for money.

"Return Monday," he said brusquely.

The sculptor was aghast at this unfriendly treatment. He returned to the palace for four days running, but each time was told that the Pope was engaged. On the fifth day a guard of the palace turned him away roughly, saying that he had orders not to admit the sculptor.

Michelangelo had not yet learned the changeable character of his patron, nor did he realize that Pope Julius was now so absorbed in the new St. Peter's as

The Pope paid no attention to Michelangelo's report.

well as in military plans that he was no longer interested in his tomb. The sculptor was as proud and tempestuous as the Pope, and he was angry and hurt to the depths of his being when he returned to his studio. He told a carpenter and a stonecutter who were living with him to sell everything they could, for he was leaving. Then he wrote to Pope Julius: "Most blessed Father, I have today been driven out of the palace by the orders of Your Holiness, wherefore I am informing you that from this day forward, if you wish to see me you must look elsewhere than in Rome."

He sent the letter by a messenger, mounted a horse and set out for Florence. It was not only the insult of being treated like a beggar that filled his heart with anger and despair. He knew from San Gallo that the Pope was about to lay the cornerstone of the new St. Peter's. That was the accomplishment of Bramante's scheme to win first place with Pope Julius. Michelangelo realized that Bramante was his enemy, that the architect was jealous of the Pope's interest in him and would do anything to keep him away. Roman society was permeated with intrigues and jealousies; even the assassination of enemies was common. Michelangelo had heard rumors that his life was in danger in Rome and, although there may have been no truth in the rumors, it gave him an added impulse for flight from the city.

Before he had traveled half the distance, messengers from the Pope caught up with him. Michelangelo was commanded to return to Rome at once, or suffer the Pope's anger. Julius sent assurance that all would be made right. Michelangelo refused firmly to turn back, despite the pleadings and commands of the messengers.

"I shall not return to Rome," he said arrogantly. He turned his horse and rode off on the road to Florence.

At home, Lodovico Buonarroti was horrified that his son had defied the Pope. Piero Soderini was also disturbed. Several messages came to the Signoria from the Pope demanding that Michelangelo be sent back to Rome at once. Soderini pleaded with the angry sculptor, saying that Florence could not afford to have the Pope's anger turned against the city, but Michelangelo stubbornly resisted. He had vowed he would not return to Rome and he would not go.

Then Pope Julius switched his interest from his disobedient sculptor to the conquest of cities he wanted for the papal states. He rode out of Rome at the head of his troops in his papal robes, and when he reached Perugia the ruler presented him with the keys of the city, surrendering without a fight. After organizing the city Pope Julius and the troops moved on to Bologna. Here too the Pope marched into the town without resistance, for the ruling family fled at the approach of the army.

No sooner was Julius settled in the palace than his thoughts returned to his rebellious sculptor. He sent an imperious message to the Signoria, demanding that Michelangelo come to Bologna without delay.

"Now see here, Michelangelo," Piero Soderini said to his friend. "This time you must obey the Pope's command. You have defied his orders as no one of the highest rank would dare to do. If the Pope is angry he is likely to attack Florence, and we can't afford to go to war over a sculptor."

Michelangelo submitted. Soderini sent him off with an escort and a letter of safe conduct. He also gave him a letter to his brother, Cardinal Soderini, in which he said: "This is to certify to Your Lordship that the bearer, Michelangelo, is an excellent young man and in his own art unsurpassed in Italy, perhaps in the universe. We cannot recommend him too highly; his nature is such that with good words and kindness he will do everything; one has only to show him love and treat him with kindness and he will perform things that will make the whole world wonder."

How well Soderini understood his tempestuous sculptor!

In his bitterness of spirit Michelangelo said he went "like a slave with a noose around his neck." On the other hand, he was drawn by his real liking for the changeable, emotional Pope and his desire to carve the marbles for the tomb.

When Michelangelo arrived in Bologna he went to Mass in the church of San Petronius to ask divine help for the dreaded interview and also to see the statues he had carved in his youth for his friend Aldrovandi. Several of the Pope's attendants who were in the church recognized him and urged him to present himself to Julius immediately.

Julius II looked his most majestic and unapproachable as Michelangelo forced himself to kneel humbly before him. The Pope said icily, "It was your duty to come to us, but you have waited until we came to you."

Michelangelo prayed for pardon. "Holy Father, I erred, but only because of great distress of mind, not being able to endure the degrading expulsion I was subjected to."

Julius said nothing, but frowned angrily. Then Cardinal Soderini, who had received the letter about Michelangelo, tried to improve matters. Turning to the Pope he said, "Your Holiness might overlook his fault; he did wrong through ignorance. These painters, outside their art, are like that."

The unfortunate Cardinal became the outlet for the Pope's wrath, for underneath his fierce actions he loved and admired his sculptor and did not wish to attack him at that moment.

"It is you, not I, who are insulting him," shouted Julius, beating his stick on the floor. "It is you, not he, who is the ignoramus and rascal. Get out of my sight and bad luck to you."

The servants rushed to the astounded Cardinal and pushed him out of the room. Then the Pope turned to Michelangelo, pardoned him and gave him the papal blessing.

"Don't leave Bologna, I have work for you," declared Julius.

"May I not return to carving the marbles for your tomb, Holy Father?" pleaded the sculptor.

The Pope shook his head vigorously, "No, no, Buonarroti, stop resisting me. You are to create a huge statue of me to be cast in bronze and placed over the façade of the church of San Petronius."

"But, Holy Father, I have no experience in bronze casting," cried Michelangelo.

"Then get a bronze caster and learn," said the Pope fiercely. "I will see that you have money for expenses. Find a workshop, send for assistants, and get to work. I am leaving Bologna soon."

Michelangelo gritted his teeth to keep from refusing. This was his penance for defying the Holy Father and he must see it through. As soon as his mind started to work out the great problems of the undertaking, he became absorbed with his usual intensity.

He studied the Pope wherever he was and whatever he was doing; his keen eyes and good memory stored up gestures, facial expressions, and actions of the vigorous body. At brief intervals Julius posed for him. At last the huge statue was completed, molded in clay over a wooden frame three times life size. Julius came to give his approval. He was pleased, but seemed to be puzzled by the uplifted right hand.

"Is my hand raised to bless or to condemn?" he asked.

Michelangelo retorted with a gleam of humor in his eyes. "Holy Father, your hand is lifted to tell the Bolognese people to behave themselves or you will punish them."

The Pope chuckled over that remark. Then he gave the sculptor his blessing, an order on a bank for funds, and left the city.

Michelangelo had found a large, bare room for a workshop with a courtyard where he built a great brick oven in which to build fires to melt the metal for casting. He had sent for the best bronze caster in Tuscany. For weeks the two men labored like slaves in the burning heat of summer, made worse by the fires. The mold was made around the clay model, the molten bronze was poured into the mold. But when it had cooled, only part of the statue came out. The whole thing had to be done over again with more weeks of weary toil and of waiting for the metal to cool. At last the statue emerged from the mold in perfect condition. Michelangelo and one helper then spent a long time polishing the bronze.

When the huge statue was finally raised to its place above the façade of San Petronius, the sculptor did not join in the celebration over the event. He was exhausted, he had only a few florins left, he longed for home. In the autumn of 1508 he left for Florence.

The great statue of Pope Julius II was seen by admiring people for only a few years. In 1511 the exiled ducal government returned to Bologna and the statue was pulled down. The bronze was melted and cast into a mighty cannon to use against the papal forces. Cannon, like church bells, used to be given names. The Duke called his cannon "The Julia."

CHAPTER 10

THE SCULPTOR CREATES FRESCOES

Once more, after a brief rest at home, Michelangelo bowed before his demanding patron in the papal audience chamber. He had been summoned to Rome to undertake more work.

Julius II welcomed him warmly and praised his success with the great bronze statue in Bologna. The two powerful characters were friends again after the reconciliation in Bologna, and the sculptor's obedient

114

following of the Pope's desire with the bronze statue.

"Buonarroti, my son," said Pope Julius, "you told me you did not understand bronze casting, yet behold the magnificent statue you created. Now I shall give you a commission that will place you above all artists in Italy. I want you to paint frescoes on the ceiling of the Sistine Chapel."

For a moment Michelangelo was so appalled he could not speak. Then he exclaimed, "Holy Father, I am not a fresco painter—I am a sculptor. I beg you to let me carve the statues for your tomb."

The Pope brushed that aside with a gesture. "There is plenty of time for the tomb, but the decoration of the Sistine Chapel must be done now. You know that the walls have been painted in fresco by great artists —Pinturicchio, Botticelli, Ghirlandaio, Perugino. But the vault is bare, only painted blue with gold stars. You wanted to paint the fresco of the Battle of Cascina in Florence; now you shall paint the Twelve Apostles for me on the ceiling of the Sistine."

Bramante, the architect, supported the Pope in his wish to have Michelangelo paint the ceiling. Perhaps he had an ulterior motive, for he was definitely antagonistic to the sculptor, jealous of his friendship with the Pope, fearful that he would become a rival in architecture if he should begin designing buildings. Bramante would be glad to have Michelangelo fail on this great project. Then he would lose the admiration of Rome, and Bramante could suggest his protegé and relative, Raphael, as the painter for the Sistine Chapel. At that time Raphael was painting the Stanze, the Pope's rooms in the Vatican, with beautiful frescoes.

Michelangelo, too, thought of Raphael for the work. "Holy Father," he said "Raphael is a great painter who will produce a masterpiece for you, but I am a worker in stone. Permit me to carve marble for you."

The more the argument built up, the more obstinate did the Pope become. When Julius set his iron will on carrying through any project, there was nothing to be done. The sculptor who did not want to paint accepted the Pope's command, but he was extremely fearful. He knew so little about fresco painting; suppose he failed in this tremendous task? He would lose his reputation and the faith of the Pope in his genius. His friends would lose faith in him too, and his enemies would rejoice.

A contract was signed, giving Michelangelo an unprecedented fee for an unprecedented undertaking. He was also to have wages for five assistants.

The anxious sculptor went to look over the Sistine Chapel. It had been built by Sixtus IV, dedicated in 1483, and was intended as part of the defenses of the Vatican as well as a chapel. The interior had been left bare so that the walls might be painted with frescoes. They had been done by the greatest artists of the generation preceding Michelangelo's. Scenes from the life of Christ and of Moses were the subjects.

The walls were one hundred thirty-three feet long, and the barrel vault rose high above them to sixty-eight feet. Michelangelo looked up and up to that arched vault of the ceiling and its supports. He not only had to paint frescoes at that height, but the problems of foreshortening and perspective in the figures would be immense.

"Lord, help me," he prayed.

Fortunately his good friend San Gallo was at hand to give him courage and confidence. He pointed out that the Pope was honoring him above all other artists. It was a challenge. Just let him believe that he would paint these frescoes better than anyone else and he would produce a masterpiece that would cause wonder in all who beheld it.

The Pope had promised help from the Vatican staff, and Bramante offered to build scaffolds on which the artist could work. When Michelangelo went to look at them he was horrified. Bramante had had his carpenters bore holes in the ceiling to hold ropes by which the scaffolds were slung down. What did he think would happen when these contraptions were taken down? There would be holes in the ceiling that could not be mended without botching the painting. Michelangelo asked the Pope's permission to build his own scaffolding. Bramante's slings were taken down, the holes blocked up. Michelangelo gave the ropes to his carpenter, who sold them and thus acquired a marriage dowry for his daughter.

Michelangelo designed the scaffolding as he wanted it, and engaged carpenters to build it. The platform rested on a projecting cornice and was solidly wedged against the strong wall with trestles beneath it. The platform was reached by a ladder and the whole thing could be moved when necessary. The painter could work high in the air without danger to himself or damage to the ceiling.

The more he studied the lofty ceiling the more his imagination peopled it with heroic figures from the Bible. The Pope wanted him to paint the Twelve Apostles in the central part of the curved vault. Michelangelo climbed the ladder to his platform to consider the great empty spaces overhead. He saw where the Apostles could be placed, but as the fire of genius burned brighter he became obsessed with the whole story of creation as told in Genesis. With great sweeps he could portray God creating heaven and earth, the sun, moon and stars, and man. He could continue his design with personalities from Genesis. Farther down he would design figures belonging to the world before Christ. The whole design would cover the ceiling down to the tops of the windows. He hurried to his workshop in the small house he had rented to sketch furiously, drawing figures and groups for the great vision he had in his mind.

In the garden of his house he had assembled the precious marbles he had brought from the Carrara quarries so long ago for the statues of Julius' tomb. His workmen friends had transported them from the meadow where they had lain neglected; some were damaged, others broken. He looked at them lovingly, for the monumental tomb was beginning to haunt his life, as it would for years to come. Sometime, somehow, he would carve the splendid figures that lived in his mind, but now he must paint the story of creation.

The Pope accepted his colossal scheme with enthusiasm, but warned his artist that it would take much longer than the original plan, perhaps years. However, if the artist wanted to paint the ceiling that way, so be it.

To help in the preparation and painting of fresco, Michelangelo wrote to his friend Francesco Granacci in Florence asking if he would assemble several artists and apprentices and come to Rome to assist him. They came, friends he had known in Florence, who lived with him and set up a real fresco workshop in the chapel. They were a great help in preparing plaster, grinding color, in blowing up cartoons and transferring them to the ceiling. Michelangelo, however, always found it difficult to work with anyone. He must do everything himself. He could not proceed like a master painter, who designed and directed the work, who executed the most important part of the fresco himself and left much of the painting to assistants.

As the powerful beings of his vision developed in his mind, Michelangelo decided he must work alone. He explained his feeling to Granacci who understood his difficult friend and loved him enough to accept the dismissal without resentment. The artists were paid and sent back to Florence. Michelangelo kept only two apprentices to grind color and to mix and lay on plaster.

Then the sculptor locked the door of the chapel. He mounted the ladder to his platform close under the ceiling. He was alone with his God and the mystery of creation. Totally absorbed in the struggle to transfer his vision to the painted ceiling, the superhuman figures he was creating seemed to come alive and to take possession of him.

Day after day, week after week, and month after month the artist crouched on his lofty platform or lay on his back, reaching up his brush to paint. He allowed none to come in except the apprentices when he needed them. His servant was allowed in during the day to climb the ladder with bread and a bowl of soup. Often, overcome with fatigue, he did not go home but slept in his clothes with his boots on. Paint dripped into his hair and beard, and sprinkled his clothes. Michelangelo himself described the agony in an ironic sonnet which reads in part:

My beard turns up to heaven; my nape falls in
Fixed on my spine; my breastbone visibly
Grows like a harp, a rich embroidery
Bedews my face from brush-drops thick and thin.
My loins into my paunch like levers grind;
My buttock like a crupper bears my weight;
My feet unguided wander to and fro;
In front my skin grows loose and long; behind
By bending, it becomes more taut and straight;
Crosswise I strain me like a Syrian bow. . . .

Sometimes he had trouble with the plaster and laying on of the colors. Then he despaired and became fearful of his success. He wrote his father, "This is not my profession. I waste my time without results. God help me." God did indeed help him with the physical energy and the inspiration to continue the mighty fresco.

Michelangelo discovered that Bramante, so favored

by the Pope, had a key to the chapel. Secretly, at night, he brought Raphael in to study the artist's work. The young painter profited by these visits and strengthened his own work on the frescoes he was painting in the Pope's rooms. The change in his style showed that Raphael realized the new world of art that was opened by the frescoes of the Sistine. Later Michelangelo said contemptuously that whatever Raphael knew about art he had learned from him—a boast that, happily, was not true. Michelangelo was angered by the sneaking visits and persuaded the Pope to take the key from Bramante.

Pope Julius was the only person, except the apprentices and servant, who was admitted to the chapel while the artist was working. When the tapping of the well-known stick was heard against the locked door, Michelangelo descended from his platform and escorted his patron, much hampered by his robes, up the narrow ladder to the platform. The two friends would discuss the progress of the designs, and the Pope would look up at the swirl of figures above his head. He was too close to see them in perspective, but he realized they were wonderful creations and he trusted his artist. Nevertheless, he was always impatient to see his projects completed without delay. Too, the Pope was in his middle sixties; by the standards of the time he was an old man. He felt he might

Pope Julius looked at the swirl of figures above his head.

not have many years to live, and he was determined to see the frescoes finished before he died.

The Pope was busy with his political undertakings even while he kept an eye on the Sistine ceiling. During the years when Michelangelo toiled on the frescoes, from 1508 to 1512, Pope Julius accomplished his most brilliant achievements in arms and embassies by forcing the French armies to withdraw beyond the Alps. In Rome he was hailed as the liberator of Italy.

The paintings in the Sistine Chapel, however, would be an honor and a monument to him equal to his achievements in war and diplomacy. The Pope was nervously impatient. Each time he climbed to the platform he prodded the artist with demands to know when the ceiling would be finished.

"When I can," Michelangelo would reply patiently.

The Pope's frustration grew. One day, when the artist had replied as usual, "When I can," Julius' fiery temper exploded.

"When I can, when I can," he roared. He seized his stick and brought it down across Michelangelo's shoulders.

Equally furious, but silent, Michelangelo escorted the Pope from the chapel and went home. He began to pack his possessions, ready once more to leave

Rome in anger and resentment. There came a knock on the door and the Pope's trusted messenger presented him with a bag of five hundred gold ducats; more important, he presented the Pope's apology for the beating. An apology from the all-powerful Pope soothed Michelangelo's pride and the hurt to his feelings. He did not run away, but returned to his work in the chapel.

In 1510 the ceiling was half finished. Julius demanded that the scaffolding be taken down so he could see the paintings. There was a fiery argument in which the Pope exploded once more. He threatened to throw Michelangelo from the scaffold if he did not obey. Grimly the artist acceded to the demand. The scaffolding came down.

Pope Julius arrived with a train of the leading men in Rome—cardinals, artists, and poets—eager to see the result of two years of secret, mysterious painting. The artist was not present, but he learned that the Pope was extremely pleased and that all visitors were awed, impressed, and a little frightened by the masterpiece they saw. Word passed around Rome, throughout cities of Italy and elsewhere in Europe, that a tremendous fresco was being painted in a style that would influence the world of art.

Bramante took the opportunity to suggest to the Pope that Raphael be asked to complete the painting on the other half of the ceiling. Thus the two greatest artists in Italy would compete in the achievement that would glorify the Pope's reign.

It was then that Michelangelo's fierce pride and temper burst out in a caustic attack on Bramante before the Pope. He told Bramante what he thought of the money he was spending on building columns for the new St. Peter's that were so badly constructed they would not support its structure. It had been senseless to destroy the columns of the original church, so cherished for centuries.

Pope Julius could tolerate this attack, so similar to the fiery way he expressed himself. He also understood that a work of art could not be painted half by one artist, half by another with different style and ideas. He told Michelangelo to rebuild his scaffolding and get on with the work.

At last, in the autumn of 1512, after four years of incredible toil, the frescoes of the ceiling were completed. Pope Julius celebrated Mass in the restored Sistine Chapel on the Vigil of All Saints. The people of Rome came to see the ceiling and to marvel. They knew that a new day had dawned in art.

Michelangelo believed that painting and sculpture were a striving toward the perfection of God. He had absorbed his whole being in the mysterious symphony of the creation of the world. The story of Genesis swept across the vault in massive, tumultuous beings that seem to float in a free sky. The majestic God of the Old Testament, his arm outstretched in command, hovers over the earth, dividing water from land, creating sun, moon and stars. In the creation of man the mighty God stretches forth his arm to meet the uplifted arm of Adam, just awakening. The two hands, human and divine, almost but not quite touch. The spark of life, invisible, leaps the gap.

In other parts of the vault were pictured the creation of Eve, the fall of man, the expulsion from the Garden of Eden, Noah and the Deluge, David and Goliath, Jonah, and other Biblical characters.

The prophets of the Old Testament had their place and below them the sibyls, or prophetesses, of the ancient pagan world. Other figures show the world before the coming of Christ. Strong male figures, called "the athletes," frame the pictures.

These tremendous scenes were not flat; they were strongly modeled like sculpture, for Michelangelo had learned to sculpture with his brush and to relate the story of creation in heroic figures that move through celestial atmosphere. The intensely creative spirit of the artist had brought together the revelation of Scripture and the revelation of the ancient pagan world which had dominated men's minds throughout the Renaissance. In the four years of painful labor he had created a new style that would dominate art for centuries to come. He had revealed how suitable an instrument is the human body for the message of the divine spirit.

For four centuries since then the wonder has survived, even though the chapel has been subjected to the chances of war and other damage. Napoleon's soldiers camped in the chapel and the smoke of cooking fires darkened the paintings. Another time the walls were damaged by explosives that went off after being stored in the chapel. Part of the ceiling was shattered and one of the athletes that frame the central pictures was completely destroyed. Yet the world continues to come, to learn what man is capable of at his highest.

In the Sistine Chapel the College of Cardinals gathers when a pope has died to elect a successor. A stove pipe, stuck through a window, sends out white or dark smoke to tell the waiting world that the burning ballots have, or have not, elected a pontiff.

After the four years of voluntary imprisonment in the chapel, Michelangelo, the man and creative artist, was completely exhausted, bodily and spiritually. He had lain on his back so long with his beard tilted up to the ceiling that he could not straighten his neck and his eyes were nearly blinded from the long strain. He took refuge in the contemplation of the marbles in his

128

garden, for surely now he might carve the statues for the tomb.

Pope Julius did not long survive the triumphant completion of the Sistine ceiling. During that winter he became ill and on February 21, 1513, he died. Michelangelo, his artist, felt deserted. Despite their frictions and quarrels, the two men had understood and loved each other; they had inspired in each other great ideas.

CHAPTER 11

TOMBS FOR THE MEDICI

In the bare Roman workshop of the sculptor marble chips flew, the ring of hammer and chisel on marble went on all day as Michelangelo worked on the statue of Moses for Pope Julius' tomb. Marble dust settled on his hair, his beard and old work clothes, while his strong arms wielded the tools with furious energy and skill. The imposing seated figure of Moses, the law-giver, was emerging from the stone. Pope Julius was gone; the tomb must be finished, and

130

the sculptor had a new contract with the Della Rovere heirs for completion of the work.

The new Pope, Leo X, was Giovanni de' Medici, a son of Lorenzo the Magnificent. He and Michelangelo had been boys together in the Medici palace. He liked music and laughter and had the Medici liking for art. But he preferred the gentle, gracious Raphael, who painted with such serene beauty, to the stormy Michelangelo. For a time the sculptor was left in peace.

The Medici family, with the power of Pope Leo X to back them, were employing every means to gain power. Giuliano, another son of Lorenzo, became governor of Florence; and his cousin, Cardinal Giulio, was also a Medici.

Pope Leo decided after a while that the Medici family must be glorified with works of sculpture, and who could do it better than the great sculptor who was highly honored in Florence? Pope Leo conceived the idea of a façade of marble figures for the Medici church of San Lorenzo in Florence. He commanded Michelangelo to leave work on the Moses and go at once to Florence to design the façade. Michelangelo protested. He begged the Pope to permit him to continue the statues for the tomb, to complete the contract.

"No, Buonarroti," said the Pope. "After all, you

are a Florentine, you were like an adopted son to Lorenzo the Magnificent; you must work for the Medici." The Pope declared he would deal with the Della Rovere heirs, and he did. He forced them to give the sculptor a new contract for a tomb of smaller dimensions, fewer figures, and nine years to complete the work. Sorrowfully Michelangelo tore himself away from this project he had dreamed of so long.

He went to Florence, took his measurements, and made a small wooden model of the façade with the figures modeled in wax. In the quarries of Carrara he was selecting blocks of marble for the work when the Pope sent word that Carrara marble would not do. He must use marble from Serravessa in Florentine territory. Undoubtedly this was part of the Medici scheme to dominate Florence and enrich its territory.

Michelangelo was in despair. It was necessary to lay out new roads and supervise their construction to get the marble from the almost inaccessible hills to the sea. The strength and time of a great artist was wasted on this work. Then, when a few blocks had been delivered in Florence, the changeable Pope had lost interest in the façade. Michelangelo was informed that the marble he had in Florence would be used to pave the floor of Il Duomo, which was badly in need of repair.

This was an insulting blow for the creative artist

who had been forced to leave the work he wanted to do in order to produce another work of art, then had the order cancelled with the contemptuous remark that the marble would be used to pave the floor of the Cathedral!

Michelangelo had a house in Florence which had been assigned to him for the work on the façade of San Lorenzo. Long ago he had stored in Florence some blocks of marble to work on, sometime, for the tomb. These had been transported to his studio, and he began to rough out four Captives that were part of the design. The work went slowly, for the artist had suffered too many disappointments, too much mistreatment. He had fallen into the mood of frustration that artists must often suffer from. No longer did he feel the divine frenzy of creation when the spirit of God seemed to guide his sculptor's hand. He was dissatisfied with his carving; he felt that he could never achieve the perfection he had in mind.

It was a period in his life when he felt that time was going too fast. He was forty-three years old. He had a record of unfinished contracts: the Piccolomini statues, the Battle of Cascina fresco, and now the unfinished statues for the tomb of Pope Julius, his friend. He was earning nothing, and money given him for the Medici work had been spent in getting the marble from Serravessa.

In bitterness of spirit he wrote to Sebastian del Piombo, his representative in Rome, telling of his despair over the Medici contract. He said: "I am not putting on the bill the wooden model of the façade that I sent to Rome. I have not put on the bill the three years I wasted on it; I have not put on the bill the fact that I have been ruined by the San Lorenzo undertaking. I have not put on the bill the great harm done to my reputation in asking me to do this work and then taking it away from me, nor do I yet know why. I have not put on the bill the damage to my house in Rome, which I had to leave and where I have lost in marbles, tools, and work already done more than 500 ducats. . . . Let us come to terms: let Pope Leo assume the cost of the work already started and the marble that has been quarried, and I shall take what remains, and then let me be free." Free—to follow his own will, to work as he wished, not to be subject to unpredictable patrons.

Pope Leo, however, did not free the artist. He and Cardinal Giulio decided to have their artist honor the Medici family by designing the Laurentian Library and the new sacristy, or Medici Chapel, of the church of San Lorenzo. In the chapel the sculptor was to design sculptures for the Medici tombs. Originally it was planned to have tombs for Lorenzo the Magnificent, his brother Giuliano, and the current rulers of the Medici. In the course of years the project dwin-

He worked in the icy atmosphere of winter.

dled down to the group of Madonna and Child; the tombs of Lorenzo, Duke of Urbino; of Giuliano, Duke of Nemours; and the wonderful figures of Night and Day, Dawn and Dusk on their tombs.

In the Medici Chapel, Michelangelo worked on the architecture and design in the icy atmosphere of winter, so that he was frequently ill. Granacci and his few other friends were greatly worried about him. Never had they seen him so sad, so morose, so shut away from friendship. He refused to join in any social gatherings, for the mood of despair was still on him. He took care of his family, helped Buonarroto with jobs, provided his aging father with money for impractical schemes. Aside from that he lived and worked alone. Some friends wrote to the Pope that their artist was not long for this world unless he was released from his labors. Pope Leo urged the artist to come to Rome for a rest, but he refused to go.

In 1521 Pope Leo died and was succeeded by Adrian VI, who lived only a year. Then the Medici, Cardinal Giulio, was elected as Pope Clement VII. During the thirty years of Medici rule of the Church, the Christian religion in Germany, Britain, Switzerland, Scandinavia, and parts of France began for the first time to be practiced as separate from the ultimate authority of Rome. This was the continent-wide movement known as the Reformation. The Popes, so occupied with developing the fortunes of the Medici, seemed hardly aware of the cataclysmic changes that were taking place in their world.

Pope Clement VII and the Emperor of the Holy Roman Empire, Charles V, had been bickering, fighting, and arranging alliances against each other for some years. In Florence at the same time, the anti-Medici Florentines were plotting revolution to drive out the Medici family.

Then the Emperor Charles V decided to move directly against the Pope. A vast imperial army, recruited from Germany, the Lowlands and Spain, invaded Italy, advancing on Rome from north and south.

In the spring of 1527 Rome was taken by the Emperor's army. Pope Clement took refuge in the city's fortress, Castel Sant' Angelo, but was able to hold out for only a month. He surrendered and was held prisoner in the Castel. Disguised as a peddler, the resourceful Clement escaped to his fortified town of Orvieto. The imperial soldiers began a brutal campaign of looting and destruction. Death, ruined houses, fire, and plague tormented the population. It was the worst disaster that had come to Rome since the ancient invasions of barbarians.

While these political turmoils were going on, Michelangelo, hidden in the chapel, worked intensively on the figures for the Medici tombs. He was roused from his absorption by the disaster to Rome and the plans of the revolutionary Florentines.

They saw their chance, with Pope Clement in the power of the Emperor Charles. Soon after the capture of Rome the revolt broke out against the Medici, and members of the family fled from the city. A Republic was proclaimed, and Michelangelo came out of his isolation to join the rebels.

However, pro-Medici factions fought the republicans to gain possession of the Palace of the Signoria. All sorts of heavy objects such as tables, benches, and chairs were thrown out the windows to drive back the pro-Medici faction.

One of these objects hit the beautiful statue of David standing before the entrance of the Palace. The left arm snapped off and fell to the pavement. Michelangelo rushed from the building to the rescue of the child of his spirit, but there was nothing to be done. It was many years before the arm was restored.

The citizens did not have long to rejoice in their Republic. In Rome the plague decimated the soldiers of the imperial army so that Emperor Charles moved out of the city with his troops and went on to attack Naples. Refugees came from Rome to Florence, bringing the plague with them. People died by the hundreds. Michelangelo's favorite brother, Buonarroto, died in his arms. He left a wife, a daughter Cecca, and a son Lionardo. Michelangelo became their guardian and undertook the expense of their education, although they continued to live with their mother. The father, Lodovico, was in Settignano at the time and so escaped the plague.

The Florentines learned that Pope Clement had sought out the Emperor and made an alliance with him in order to regain his position in Rome. The republicans of Florence realized that the Pope would soon move to attack Florence with his own and the imperial troops to regain the city for the Medici. They set up their government with a Council of Eighty, preparing for trouble.

Michelangelo, always republican in spirit, was heart and soul with the defenders of a free Florence. He felt no loyalty or liking for the current, unworthy descendants of his friend and patron, Lorenzo the Magnificent. They were self-indulgent, power-loving men of small minds. He loved his city and would defend it. He became a member of the Council and was given charge of repairing the fortifications of the city.

Those men of genius in the Renaissance period used their capacities to the full in many fields. Leonardo da Vinci was engineer and designer of fortifications, an inventor and scientist besides being a great painter. Michelangelo had proved his ability as sculptor, fresco painter, and architect. He now turned his keen mind and his knowledge of stone to the problem of fortifications.

The mood of despair was gone; he felt once more the vigor and invention of earlier years. When Florence needed him, it was no time for sculpture. Michelangelo locked the Medici Chapel and gave the key to a friend who wanted a safe place to store valuables. He was appointed Governor-General of Fortifications and devoted himself to the defense of his city.

CHAPTER **12**

IN DEFENSE OF FLORENCE

Florentines reacted to the danger from the Pope's army with enthusiasm as they prepared defenses. A citizens' militia went into training to provide the best hope for resistance to the overwhelming superiority of the enemy's troops. Michelangelo spent days studying the city's defense walls and the towers for cannon. They were in bad repair. He had no knowledge, from a military point of view, of how to protect the city walls from enemy cannon, but since he had worked with stone all his life, he could judge the strength of

141

stones and the best methods of building fortifications with them. Military engineering was not particularly complicated in the sixteenth century. Michelangelo set out to learn what he needed to know by a visit to Ferrara, whose Duke was reported to have built the best defenses in northern Italy.

The Duke of Ferrara received him gladly, hoping to keep him in the city to produce sculpture for him. After being taken on a tour of the fortifications, however, Michelangelo insisted he must return to Florence where he was needed. He cheerfully promised to create sculpture for the Duke in the future.

The new supervisor of fortifications went to work at once in Florence with a crew of laborers to strengthen the walls and dig ditches into which attackers would fall. He looked over the surrounding countryside to choose the most efficient vantage point for defense.

Florence, on the Arno River, is lower than much of the country around it, a distinct disadvantage. Michelangelo planned to fortify the neighboring district of San Miniato on higher ground, where there was an old church and a strong, ancient tower. That would be an ideal location for watching enemy movements. Troops approaching the city could be fired on from San Miniato.

In this atomic age, military science can destroy a city from the air with a few atomic bombs; and walls, if there were any, would be no protection from an enemy approaching by air. There was a different system of attack and defense in Michelangelo's day. Cities were usually taken by siege. The attackers marched toward their goal, and in the process people of the countryside often took refuge within the walls of the city. On the approach of the enemy, the city gates would be closed and soldiers would man the walls.

The attacking troops would hurl great stones over the walls, both to kill defenders and make breaches in the walls. The defenders would retaliate by shooting cannon, or by attacking whole units as they reached the walls with great stones, hot lead, and boiling water. Cannon balls were nothing like artillery shells of the present time. They were hardly more than man-made rocks thrown with great force, but they could knock holes in defensive walls.

The siege of Florence began as troops of the Pope and the Emperor camped on surrounding hills. Their officers understood Michelangelo's scheme to use San Miniato as an outpost. He had built a wall on the hill and installed cannon, but the enemy concentrated fire on the tower which they realized was a lookout. Day after day their cannon boomed, and the ancient tower shook under direct hits. Stones tumbled from the walls.

Michelangelo studied the situation. The tower

143

must be repaired. He sent out messengers to collect masons and stonecutters to refit the stones and re-plaster the walls. They toiled all night, but cement in the repaired walls needed time to harden or cannon balls would knock holes once more. The artist looked up at the wide cornice at the top of the tower that ex-tended some way out from the walls. If pads of some sort were hung from the cornice, cannon balls might be deflected. Why not try mattresses?

He sent messengers through the town demanding mattresses from homes and sacks of wool from the wool shops. All these thick pads were suspended by ropes from the cornice, from which they hung down over the walls. When the bombardment began again the cannon balls struck the heavy padded sacks and fell into the ditch below without doing harm. Michel-angelo's scheme was original and ingenious, and the success of it won him high praise from the citizens.

Meanwhile the citizens' militia needed a command-ing officer, and there was no one at hand for the post. The Council asked General Malatesta Baglioni from Perugia to take command of the militia and to bring some of his soldiers. Michelangelo was distressed at this move. The General did not have a good repu-tation as a fighting leader. The two men became en-emies at once. As supervisor of defenses Michelangelo ventured to criticize some of Malatesta's acts. The militia was badly organized and not eager to fight;

Malatesta was careless and indifferent. Not for a moment did Michelangelo trust the General. His behavior was suspicious. There were whispers of disloyalty and treachery throughout the town as some citizens and some soldiers were suspected. People friendly to the Medici were intriguing for their return, and there was dissension among various groups of civic leaders. Michelangelo was convinced that Malatesta would betray the city. When he told his suspicions to the gonfalonier, Francesco Carducci, he made no impression. Carducci was an honest man but weak and credulous.

"You are mistaken, Michelangelo," he said. "I'm sure of General Malatesta's loyalty and it won't be long now. The imperial army is disorganized, many men are sick with the plague. They will give up soon and I expect victory for Florence."

Naturally, Michelangelo's complaints reached the ears of General Malatesta, who hated this man for his criticism and interference. The General was all-powerful in Florence. If he decided to get rid of Michelangelo, the city was no safe place for him. Presently a friend, supposed to be one of the Council, came to him secretly.

"You must leave at once," he said. "Malatesta is plotting against you. I will provide horses, but be sure to leave tonight."

This news added to the sculptor's fears for Flor-

Michelangelo's scheme was ingenious.

ence. He was sure that Malatesta intended to betray the city; he saw no hope for Florentines to regain their liberty. He could not prevent the disaster, and with the Medici in control he probably would be arrested. He decided to leave.

Escape had been a pattern in this artist's life. Several times, when he was in a situation where he feared for his physical safety and his opportunity to work at art, he had taken refuge in flight. He had run from Florence after the death of Lorenzo; from Rome after the Pope expelled him from the audience chamber and he thought enemies were plotting to assassinate him. Now he fled again from Florence because his life was in danger.

With two companions he escaped through an unguarded gate and started for Venice. His companions thought better of their flight and returned to Florence. Michelangelo went to Venice, but he was not content to stay there, although the Venetian people welcomed him. He thought of going to France, to the kingdom of Francis I, as Leonardo had done when Italy disappointed him.

In Florence the flight of their great citizen and general of the fortifications caused a sensation. The Council ordered that all deserters would be treated as rebels, their property confiscated unless they returned by a certain date. Michelangelo's friends begged leniency for him. They sent messengers urging the artist to return. The Council promised to pardon him, although he must lose his seat in the government for three years.

In a spirit of shame and penitence, Michelangelo returned. His flight had been a mad impulse to escape everything that threatened him, and he regarded it as cowardice. He took up his work at San Miniato to help the city through the siege that was becoming worse day by day. The citizens deliberately destroyed houses and crops outside the walls in a sort of "scorched earth" policy to keep supplies from reaching the besieging army, but it injured their own food supply as well.

At night the sculptor turned from his defense work to lock himself into the Medici Chapel to work steadily on the statues. He carved by the light of a candle attached to his hat, as he had done before.

The city was not attacked, but the enemy found means to reduce the spirits of the defenders by cutting off food supplies. The siege had gone on for a long time; the will to fight had weakened, and in the hot summer of 1530 people were dying of hunger, the plague, and lack of water.

In August, General Malatesta betrayed the Florentines. The gates were opened to the army of the Pope and the Emperor. Alessandro de' Medici, a vicious, cruel young man, became governor of Florence. Reprisals began as republicans were hunted down, arrested, and executed. Some of Michelangelo's best friends were put to death. The artist was saved from a like fate by the priest of the little church of San Niccolo altr' Arno who hid him in the belfry and brought him food. Many people knew where their artist was hidden but they would not tell the government.

Pope Clement, after accomplishing his aim to restore the Medici as rulers of Florence, was in a more kindly mood. He thought of the sculptor and of the unfinished statues in the Medici Chapel. He asked friends in Florence to find the sculptor, assure him he would be safe if he would return to work on the statues. He sent money to the prior of San Lorenzo and ordered him to treat the sculptor with every consideration.

What could this Florentine artist do but accept the Pope's offer? The city was his home; the unfinished sculptures weighed on his mind and conscience. Through another long, cold winter he labored with intensity on the statues. He was thin and sick, he could not eat when he should, nor would he take enough time for sleep. He was driven by the urge to complete this work he had promised to the unworthy Medici who had conquered his city, but there was no joy in it. Francesco tried to help him, urging him not to kill himself with work but to visit with his artist friends occasionally.

149

Pope Clement was really fond of Michelangelo in his own way and tried, during his last few years, to be a friend to the sculptor. He asked him to come to Rome for a rest, but once again the sculptor refused to leave Florence until the statues were finished.

When the Medici Chapel was completed, all those who saw the magnificent sculptures acclaimed them as the height of perfection in Michelangelo's career. This was true, and the sculptor knew it, but he could not feel the old-time, proud satisfaction in his creative work. Throughout the long turmoil of frenzied labor his spirit had been sunk in the depths of anguish—sorrow for the loss of liberty to Florence, and to Italy which had become a pawn in the rivalry between Francis I of France and Emperor Charles V; despair over the failure of mankind to rise above the cruelties of war and politics, or to live with humane spirit and high principles. He also despaired of any future for himself.

In the small, classical chapel there is a tomb on each side. They were the only two of the original plan that were completed, and they honored two minor personalities: Lorenzo, Duke of Urbino, and Giuliano, Duke of Nemours. Michelangelo made no effort to portray the men as they were. His splendid sculptures symbolize two contrasting elements that were always important in his life—Action and Contemplation. Giuliano, dressed as a Roman commander,

The tremendous task was completed.

seems to accept the responsibility of all human actions; Lorenzo, his face shaded by a great helmet, is
plunged into deep thought. Face and figure cast
doubt on the worth of any action.

A carved sarcophagus stands below each Medici
statue, crowned with wonderfully modeled figures
whose faces express doubt and despair: Dusk and
Dawn below the figure of Contemplation, Day and
Night below that of Action. Together they represent
the unbearable tragedy of human life as Michelangelo
then felt it. Before the altar stands a strong, beautiful

151

statue of the Madonna holding her Child. Her face expresses serene acceptance in the face of divine destiny.

Michelangelo was aware of the resignation, almost the despair, that radiates from the great sculptures. During his days of torment he had found relief in writing poems on the back of drawings. Of the Night he wrote:

"Sweet is my sleep, but more to be mere stone,
  so long as ruin and dishonor reign;
To hear naught, to feel naught, is my great gain;
Then wake me not, speak in an undertone."

The tremendous task was completed; the beautiful figures were ready to be put in position. Michelangelo gave instructions to his assistants to do this; then he left the chapel, a free man but one who was exhausted in body and spirit.

At this time his aging father, ill and senile, died on his ninetieth birthday. The old man had loved his son in his fractious way, and Michelangelo had been devoted to his father in spite of his complaints and criticisms. He had loved his ungrateful family and had taken care of them to the best of his ability. There was nothing to hold him in the city now. It was no longer the vivid, alive Florence of his youth, nor was it the creative center of beauty and art it had been under Lorenzo the Magnificent. His city was ruled by unworthy men, it was filled with deceit and intrigue.

A message from Pope Clement gave him the excuse to leave. The Pope urged Michelangelo to come to Rome, to recuperate from his labors and to discuss new work. The sculptor was now sixty years old. At the moment he did not know what to do with the remaining years of life. He might as well try Rome. He settled his affairs in Florence; he packed up on mules some possessions and his precious tools. Accompanied by his young servant, Urbino, he rode out from the gate of Florence. On September 23, 1534, the great Florentine artist said farewell forever to his dearly beloved city, for he never returned.

CHAPTER **13**

THE LAST JUDGMENT

The return to Rome brought no happiness to the ailing artist. His strong body, driven to superhuman labor for so long by the power of his will, was worn out. He felt old, his bones creaked, there were streaks of gray in his rough hair and beard. He and the young Urbino settled into the shabby old house he had left behind when he departed from Rome. It had been ransacked by thieves, but nothing in his workshop was damaged.

There stood the Moses nearly finished, and other blocks of marble with rough forms emerging from the stone. He would stay in the studio with the memory of Julius, Michelangelo decided, and at last he would finish the work that had weighed on his spirit so long.

Urbino fussed over his master with loving care. He shopped for food and prepared tasty meals to tempt the artist's appetite. He tried to make the rough old house comfortable, but he was worried by the artist's lack of spirit.

"Do not be sad, Master," he said. "Your friends will soon come to see you."

"I have no friends, nor do I want any," was the gloomy reply.

At that time the great artist did indeed feel that he was alone. His father and brothers were gone; he had no family left except his nephew Lionardo, who had wife and children. There were few friends he cared about except Francesco Granacci in Florence. Giuliano da San Gallo, the architect with whom he had planned a chapel for Julius' tomb, had died and his son, Antonio da San Gallo, was now working for the Pope. Jacopo Galli, who had given the artist, when young, his friendship and counsel, was long since gone. Great artists whom he had admired, though not as friends, had died: Leonardo da Vinci in France and Raphael, at the age of thirty-seven, in Rome.

The artists of Italy, as well as many other people who admired and liked him, called him "the divine Michelangelo." They were always ready to help him, but there were others who disliked him because of his rough manners, pride, and caustic tongue. Yet this stormy man always had great capacity for love. He had wanted friends, but found it difficult to maintain affectionate relations with other people. He had lavished love and care on his unresponsive family; he had helped many poor people, had liked and helped workmen he knew. Most of his emotions had found outlet in his intense love of beauty in all forms and in his deep religious feeling. Now he gave affection to Urbino whom he had trained to be servant, secretary, and sometimes helper in his work.

Urbino asked him, "You are going to work on the Moses, Master?"

"Yes, I am, but first I must visit the Pope who sent for me."

He had only one interview with Pope Clement, who asked him to compose a mighty fresco of the Last Judgment for the altar wall of the Sistine Chapel. Then, in a few days, the Pope died.

The sculptor gladly shut himself up in the workshop with the Moses. With loving skill he chiseled and polished each fold of drapery, the strong hands holding the tablets of the Law, the imposing head

156

with stern eyes and mouth and long, curling beard. With every delicate touch of tools on the face he added something of Julius—the keen mind, the force and judgment.

He made no effort to see the new Pope, Paul III, who was a member of the ancient Farnese family of Rome. Paul III was a man Michelangelo could like. He was another Julius in his personal, direct, forceful way of setting goals and going after them. Paul III was like Julius, too, through his interest in works of art, in his determination to make Rome a worthy capital of Christendom. The great sculptor must work for him.

It was not long before Michelangelo was summoned to an audience at the Vatican. He knelt to kiss the papal ring, then listened to the Pope's request that he continue on the plan for the Last Judgment fresco that Pope Clement had wanted.

"Holy Father," the sculptor protested, "I must explain to you that I am bound under contract to finish the tomb of Julius II. The Della Rovere heirs are demanding that I finish the statues without delay. They are threatening to sue me."

Michelangelo must have felt that he had spent days of his life explaining to one Pope that he was bound by contract to earlier Popes. Paul III responded with a vigor that was reminiscent of Julius.

"I have waited thirty years to have you in my service. Now that I am Pope, can't I have my wish? As to the contract, bring it to me and I'll tear it up."

The sculptor bowed submissively and returned to his house in a confused state of mind. A few days later there was a knock at the door. When Urbino opened it, two Swiss Guards from the Vatican stood there bringing the announcement that the Pope was on his way to visit the sculptor.

"Master," said Urbino, his eyes round with astonishment, "the Pope is coming to visit! What shall we do —the studio is so dirty."

"We shall receive him with courtesy just as we are," said the sculptor firmly. "This is an artist's studio, not a palace."

When the Pope arrived, splendid in papal robes, accompanied by a group of scarlet-robed cardinals, the sculptor in dusty work clothes welcomed him with simple dignity. The visitors inspected with interest the tools and marbles of the studio. Michelangelo led the Pope to the statue of Moses.

"This is the Moses for the Julius tomb, Your Holiness. This is the sculpture that is keeping me busy now."

The Pope and the cardinals walked around the massive statue, inspecting it closely, exclaiming over its beauty and strength. One cardinal said to the Pope, "Your Holiness, that statue alone suffices to honor the

He asked to see the sketches for the Last Judgment.

memory of Julius II or that of any other great man."

"You are right," agreed the Pope.

Then he asked to see the sketches Michelangelo had begun for the Last Judgment before Pope Clement died. The drawings, full of vigor and action, pleased the Pope very much. He smiled understandingly at the sculptor.

"Buonarroti, I know you are eager to finish this fine work of art, the Moses. But I want you to proceed with the cartoon drawings for the Last Judgment, and when that is finished we shall study the chapel to decide how to use the altar wall. Leave the Della Roveres to me," he added. "I will see that you are released to paint the fresco."

This Pope was one who did not forget his promises. The Della Roveres had to bow to his will and agree to another contract. The once monumental tomb planned by Pope Julius and Michelangelo was to be reduced to the Moses and two other statues, Leah and Rachel, representing Action and Contemplation. The sculptor was released to paint the fresco before finishing the Julius statues.

For the second time the sculptor turned from his cherished work in marble to paint frescoes. His mind, relieved from the Della Rovere threats, concentrated on designs for the colossal groups of figures that would fill the wall of the Sistine Chapel. Innumerable drawings and compositions littered the studio.

At this time the lonely life of the artist was brightened by the warmest, most satisfying friendships he had known. Once before, on a visit to Rome, he had met the young nobleman of a patrician Roman family, Tommaso dei Cavaliere. The marvelous beauty of the young man had remained in his memory as an example of Greek perfection—his supple, slender body, beautiful head and finely chiseled features.

Now, in Rome, the old artist and young patrician renewed their acquaintance. Michelangelo discovered that physical beauty was only part of the irresistible charm of this young man. Tommaso had a serious intellectual quality; he was an architect and was devoted to all forms of art. A deep affection grew between the two men as they became close companions. Together they studied the splendid ruins of Rome's former grandeur. They made architectural drawings of the reconstruction they thought was possible on the finest ruinous buildings. In one studio or another they worked together. Michelangelo gave his young friend lessons in drawing, as he assured him that perfection of draughtsmanship was the basis of all art. He gave Tommaso priceless drawings of his own for his collection. They discussed the cartoon the artist was making for the great Sistine fresco.

One day Tommaso said to his friend, "There is a wonderful woman I want you to meet. She is Vittoria Colonna, widow of the Marquis of Pescara. She is noted as the most famous woman in Italy for her intellect, her poetry, and her devotion to the Church. I am fortunate to be counted as one of her circle of friends."

"She would see nothing in me—a rough, crotchety old sculptor," replied Michelangelo.

"Dear friend, you are 'the divine Michelangelo' whose genius is honored by everyone," Tommaso said affectionately.

Tommaso took his friend, on the next Sunday afternoon, to the gardens of the convent of San Silvestre al Quirinale, where Vittoria Colonna met her friends each week. In the shady garden were gathered some of the most liberal-minded scholars, churchmen, and artists of Italy. Vittoria Colonna, by the radiance of her personality, her intellect and piety, was the stimulating center of the group. She gave her hand to Michelangelo with the words, "Welcome, my friend. I have known your genius and your works for years."

The group discussed everything from poetry and philosophy to the needs for reform within the Church. That was Vittoria Colonna's chief concern at the time. She gathered around her and wrote to the leaders of the Church who were thinking, as she was, of plans for reform. One of these leaders was Cardinal Pole of England, who was her friend and her spiritual director. He was trying to persuade Henry VIII of

162

The group discussed everything.

England not to leave the Catholic Church to found the Church of England.

Tommaso and Michelangelo went many times to the gatherings at San Silvestre. The friendship between the sculptor and the saintly woman of high ideals became happy and idyllic. Michelangelo made beautiful drawings for her, and she presented him with her book of poems. Under her stimulation the sculptor returned to writing poetry. He composed many sonnets and madrigals dedicated to Vittoria Colonna. Her serene faith, which rose above all human failures, helped him to surmount his doubts and to return to his belief in the power and love of God.

So it was that, in his sixties, a period of joyous friendship and warm affection came to the troubled artist. He had warmth at home, too, for Urbino married a girl of his village and brought her to live at the sculptor's house. His wife gave Michelangelo motherly care. When a son was born the parents named him Michelangelo, and the sculptor held the baby at his baptism. The affection and stimulation of his friends made this period of the artist's life seem like a glorious sunset after a stormy day.

The huge cartoon for the Sistine wall was finished and approved. Then the Pope issued an edict that Michelangelo Buonarroti was appointed Chief Architect, Painter and Sculptor to the Apostolic Palace.

The Pope and the artist conferred on the problem

of preparing the altar wall. It was not bare of decoration, for Perugino had painted frescoes which were dim from time and candle smoke. Above the windows were paintings by Michelangelo himself. He decided to remake the whole wall. Neither he nor the Pope hesitated to destroy frescoes already there. It was often done while remodeling buildings. The windows were blocked up, the wall was rebuilt, slanting outward slightly from the vertical.

Michelangelo's friend, the painter Sebastiano del Piombo, was to assist him, and he was given the task of preparing the surface of the wall for painting. He prepared it for oil painting, so popular at the time, perhaps in the belief that the old artist would want the latest method in painting. He could not have been more mistaken. Michelangelo took one look at the wall and gave orders that the surface was to be removed and replaced by the traditional rough plaster for fresco. He could not forget what had happened to Leonardo's splendid mural of the Battle of Anghiara in the Great Hall at Florence. Sebastiano lost his chance to help on the painting.

Scaffoldings were built, so that once more the artist must scramble up and down ladders and crouch on platforms. The muscles and joints of a man in his sixties did not have the resilience of those of the younger man who had painted the Sistine ceiling. Almost a quarter of a century had passed since he had finished that great painting. The new one was grueling work, but the artist was so absorbed in his vision of the Judgment Day that he worked hours on end, day after day. Urbino helped him with the plaster and preparation of colors.

Hard as it was, the work of painting was not the lonely agony of the years he had spent on the ceiling. Now he had the companionship of his two friends, Tommaso and Vittoria Colonna, in the hours he took from work. They discussed the progress of the fresco, the meaning of the overwhelming scene he was painting, and their belief in him helped to build up his confidence. Paul III was also constant in his interest and encouragement. There was friendship between the Pope and his artist; indeed, this Pope was devoted to Michelangelo. Paul's protection was to be valuable against the criticism of enemies in the future.

Michelangelo spent five years on the Last Judgment, from 1536 to 1541. Into the design, tremendous in scope, of swirling figures rising and falling he poured the culmination of a lifetime of thought and question on the relation of mankind with God. He put into the terrifying scene the judgment of God on the evils of human living as he saw it in the world around him—the luxury, godlessness, the political trickery, and useless wars for power. He turned from his former love of Greek beauty and philosophy to the austere feeling of earlier years when he had nourished his mind on constant reading of Dante's *Divine Comedy* and the Old Testament, when he had listened to the fiery preaching of Savonarola. His conception of Judgment Day reflected the uncompromising severity of the monk's ideas.

The wrath of God, the judgment on mankind for their sins, he painted into the stern, massive figure of the Christ with one arm uplifted as though to strike. The swirling clouds of bodies, the dead called from their graves by the trumpet announcing the Day of Judgment, the saints and prophets, the condemned— all rise and fall as though in whirlwinds around this central figure, and the condemned tumble headlong down to hell.

When the fresco was nearly finished Pope Paul insisted on seeing it. He stared at the awe-inspiring scene, then fell on his knees and prayed, "Lord, be merciful to me in Thy judgment." When he rose he blessed Michelangelo and the fresco.

The artist needed support and protection from the Pope after High Mass was celebrated in the chapel on All Hallows Eve, 1541. The people who looked at the tremendous painting back of the altar were overwhelmed, terrified—so much so that they could not appreciate the magnificent conception and execution of the painting. There were criticisms that grew into a storm, as many viewers were scandalized that in this scene of judgment the artist had painted most figures, some of them saints and angels, completely without clothing.

To Michelangelo the human body was capable of the highest expression of emotion and thought. He could not conceive of clothing on souls called to the judgment of God. It never occurred to him that his presentation would shock people as indecent and irreverent in a holy place where Mass was celebrated. He refused to touch the painting, and the Pope supported him. Throughout Rome enemies circulated reports of the scandalous painting Michelangelo had created. There were demands that the fresco be scraped off or painted over, but the Pope commanded that the wall must not be touched.

Energetic Pope Paul wanted to keep his artist at work, tired though he was. He begged Michelangelo to paint frescoes in his Pauline Chapel, just finished. Wearily, the artist agreed but did not undertake the work until a year later, for he had a serious illness after his long labor.

The period of calm and serenity was over for the artist who had spent most of his life in conflict. Cardinal Caraffa was in favor of the Congregation of the Holy Inquisition which he was trying to introduce into Italy from Spain. Outspoken believers in reform within the Church came under suspicion, and many were accused of heresy. Vittoria Colonna was under suspicion because she was drawn into the controversy concerning justification by faith. Her house was searched and, after being questioned, she left Rome to take refuge in a convent at Viterbo. Only the Pope's protection saved Michelangelo from the same danger. Therefore he lost the inspiration of Vittoria's companionship, although they corresponded constantly and exchanged poems.

One satisfaction came to the artist, who had been haunted and frustrated for years over the Julius tomb. He finished the figures of Leah and Rachel, which were to be companions to the Moses. In 1545 the statues were placed in the small church of San Pietro in Vinculi to honor Pope Julius II. Although the monumental tomb conceived by the Pope and Michelangelo was an unfulfilled dream, the artist was at last free of the burden he had carried for so long.

CHAPTER **14**

THE DOME OF ST. PETER'S

A weary old man laid down his brushes and
stepped back to look at his frescoes in the Pauline
Chapel. The scaffolding had been taken down, and
he was putting the finishing touches on the lower part
of the paintings. Tommaso dei Cavaliere stood beside
Michelangelo studying the Martyrdom of St. Peter
on one wall, the Conversion of St. Paul on the other.

"Your hand has not lost its skill, dear friend, or
your mind the imaginative conception in paintings.

170

These frescoes are impressive. Pope Paul will be tremendously pleased."

The old artist stretched his cramped fingers. "I've painted my last fresco. I'm seventy years old—too old to be scrambling around on scaffolds. Pope Paul begged me to paint these frescoes and I could not refuse, because he is my friend."

"What next then—architecture?" asked Tommaso. "After you have had a little rest, suppose we continue our sketches and studies of the Roman ruins."

It was a good suggestion, one that led the way to the next request from the Pope of many ideas. Paul III and his council were planning the restoration of the Capitol, the site of government and religion in the Roman Empire. The stately buildings were in ruins.

Vitality returned to Michelangelo with the prospect of this undertaking, for he had a deep feeling for the glories of ancient Rome. He would make architectural plans for the restoration, and Tommaso, who was a good architect, would be his assistant. The two friends went to work but, as so often before, the artist's plans were delayed by the Pope himself.

Paul III certainly wished to restore architectural beauty to Rome, but more immediate was the necessity to reconstruct the fortifications of the city which had been damaged in the attack by the imperial troops in 1527. There was danger, for both French and Spanish soldiers were swarming over Italy and the

Romans feared another siege. Antonio da San Gallo, son of Michelangelo's friend Giuliano, was the papal architect. He had been supervising this work for some time. Michelangelo was asked by the Pope to look over the defenses and give his opinion.

In a meeting of the council the artist proposed different ideas from those of San Gallo and pointed out faults in construction. The criticism infuriated San Gallo, who was present and angrily told the artist to stick to his sculpture and leave fortifications alone. The two men hurled insults at each other until the Pope commanded them to stop. He ordered Michelangelo to make a new plan, and when this was submitted to the council it was accepted. San Gallo died in a short time from malaria. Then Pope Paul issued an edict appointing Michelangelo Buonarroti as governor and architect of St. Peter's, with full powers to carry on construction.

At first it seemed impossible to the aging artist to undertake this monumental task. To build St. Peter's would be the work of years, and he was an old man in his seventies. Then his mood changed. The thought of death was with him constantly; he would devote his remaining years to the service of God by building this central church of Christendom. He accepted the position but refused any pay for his services. He would work on the holy church for the love of God. He wrote his nephew Lionardo that he believed it was the divine will that he should undertake this task.

Just at this time a great grief came to him. His beloved friend, Vittoria Colonna, who had returned to Rome very ill, soon died. A light had gone out of his life. Now he had only Tommaso and a group of young artists who were his devoted pupils and assistants. They worked under his direction on the architectural restoration of Roman buildings and on St. Peter's.

Michelangelo chose to continue the design made by Bramante years before, which had been altered by San Gallo. He looked over the columns and walls already built, deciding that they must be strengthened to support the vault and dome of Bramante's design. Every day he crossed the city on his old horse to spend the day at St. Peter's. He must oversee the placing of each stone, test the mortar, keep a sharp eye on the contractor and laborers to see that there was no cheating on materials or construction as had been done under other architects. His pupils carried out his orders. Michelangelo made up his mind that he would not leave St. Peter's until the work had been brought to such a point that plans could not be changed after his death.

Duke Cosimo of Florence constantly begged him to return to his own city for the rest of his life, to rest and be honored. The Buonarroti family, because of Michelangelo's fame, now held a position of high

He decided to use Bramante's design.

rank in Florence. When the Academy of Florence was founded Michelangelo was appointed president. But the artist refused to leave Rome and St. Peter's, although he longed for his home.

It was tragic that this man of genius was obliged to spend his last years battling conspiracies by his enemies, who did everything possible to hinder him in the great work on St. Peter's. There were cardinals whose protégés with lucrative jobs on the construction were dismissed by Michelangelo because of inferior work. There were architects who resented the fact that they had to submit to the orders of this imperious genius. Contractors, who had been making unjust profits from their supplies and construction, resented him. The superintendents of finances were angered because Michelangelo would not submit his plans to them.

These enemies spread the word around Rome that Michelangelo was too old for this high position, that construction was badly done and the chief architect shut out inspectors from the area because they would see his mistakes. Their complaints to the Pope caused him to hold a hearing at which Michelangelo had to answer his critics. He came through the ordeal triumphantly, and the Pope dismissed the complaints. He told Michelangelo to continue in his own way.

Frequently the artist became ill from hard work and worry. Then Urbino and his wife tended him

175

faithfully. He said to Urbino one day, "When I die what will you do?"

"I suppose I must serve someone else, Master," Urbino replied.

"Poor fellow, I must save you from poverty," exclaimed the artist. He gave his devoted companion two thousand crowns, sufficient for him to end his days in peace.

As it happened, it was Urbino who died first. In 1555 he had a severe illness from which he did not recover. The artist wanted his widow and the little Michelangelo to stay with him, but the young woman insisted she must return to her village. The old man wrote to his nephew, "He left me so sad and troubled because of the love I had for him that it would have been easier if I had died with him." Michelangelo found a new servant, Antonio, a fellow with a good heart, who tried his best to take care of the difficult old artist.

Michelangelo began his work as Chief Architect of St. Peter's in 1547 and continued his designing and his watch over construction until a short time before his death. When Pope Paul III died in 1549 the artist considered giving up to return to Florence because he feared the new Pope would not support him. Marcellus II lived only a few months and was succeeded by Pope Julius III, who confirmed Michelangelo's position as Chief Architect. Julius III had great affection for him.

The artist's fighting spirit and his conscience would not let him resign, no matter how his enemies tormented him. That would be a move which would please them but would dishonor him as an architect. He wrote to a friend, "Now that construction is so far advanced that I can begin to vault the dome, to leave Rome would be to ruin the whole work, a great shame to me and for my soul, a great sin."

Julius III was succeeded by Paul IV, who was the Cardinal Caraffa. He was still a severe man, a strict guardian of orthodoxy, but he did not disturb Michelangelo in his position. He did demand, however, that draperies be painted on the nude figures in the fresco of the Last Judgment. The task was given to the painter Daniele Volterra, who was a friend of Michelangelo. He apologized to the master for having to do this, but assured him he would treat the painting with the greatest respect and would brush in the draperies so lightly that they could easily be painted out later on.

Although the artist's faith in his mission kept him going, his strength was failing. Tommaso and his other friends were greatly concerned because none of Michelangelo's final plans for the construction of St. Peter's were written down. They were all in his head, and he had refused to submit plans to any of the authorities. Tommaso persuaded him to work out on paper the most important designs for the structure. These he swore to protect after the artist's death, and he would not permit any changes to be made in the plans.

Tommaso also begged Michelangelo to make a wooden model of the dome, complete with every item of sculptural decoration. The artist was dreaming over his plan for the dome; it was to be as beautiful as Brunelleschi's dome over the Cathedral of Florence, but different. He began with Bramante's original plan for the classical dome, a perfect hemisphere. Then he incorporated into this ancient form, designed by pagans of Rome centuries before, some of the distinctly Christian thrust toward heaven that is so familiar in the great medieval cathedrals of northern Europe.

He mounted the dome on top of a cylinder, or drum, then elongated the dome proper. Where the vast curved surfaces came together at the top he placed still another upthrust in the form of a lantern, a cylinder of windows enclosed in columns. There was another rise in the form of curved ribs going inward. Where they came together there was a ball, symbolizing the world, and this was surmounted by a cross. The artist conceived the architecture of the whole building to lift skyward, and the dome was the culmination of this reach toward heaven. The three tiers of the dome symbolized the triple tiers of the papal crown worn by the head of the Church.

Michelangelo did not live to see the completion of

his magnificent design for the church and the dome. In later years his plans were altered somewhat by other architects, who added heavy ornamentation that lost some of the majestic simplicity of the original design, but the dome is truly his.

The solid, thrusting dome of St. Peter's Basilica has been a landmark above the city of Rome during the intervening centuries. For three hundred and fifty years that dome has marked the heart of Catholic Christianity. Beneath that huge enclosed space the Popes offer the holy sacrifice of the Mass. In that dome's shadow the succeeding heads of the Catholic Church have spoken from a balcony to the city and the world with words of love and anguish, of fatherly concern and instruction in time of danger, of disaster, or of ever-renewed hope for the future. The shape of the dome seems to encompass all the world and to lift the world upward toward heaven. Hundreds of feet below the ball and cross there stands the Pope's altar of St. Peter's. And below that, according to recent excavations, is a grave that is believed to be that of St. Peter himself.

For twenty years the great genius, Michelangelo, concentrated on his labor of love for God in the great church and its dome. In his late eighties, though he was daily weaker, he refused to stop. All day he was at St. Peter's. At night, with a candle in his hat in the old-time manner, he was at work chipping marble from a block with a hand that was losing its strength. He was carving two Pietàs. When his friends protested, he told them it made him feel healthy to work on marble. On some nights when he could not sleep, he mounted his old horse and rode through the dark streets of Rome, visiting the places that had meant so much to him.

Three weeks before his eighty-eighth birthday he spent the whole day in the studio hammering away at a final Pietà. In his last days he struggled, as he had all his life, to bring forth creative conceptions from stone. A few days later one of his friends found him wandering aimlessly in the rain, his face contorted, unable to speak. He had suffered a slight stroke. His friends put him to bed and never left him alone. He asked to have his nephew Lionardo summoned from Florence.

On February 18, 1564, two weeks before his birthday, he seemed worse. The doctors were sent for, his artist friends gathered around his bed—Tommaso, his best companion; Daniele Volterra; Giorgio Vasari and others, who were both his pupils and his fellow artists. From the Pope came Cardinal Salviati to administer the Last Sacraments.

The stormy man of genius had found peace at last and was ready for death. He turned to his friends and said, "I bequeath my soul to God; my body to the earth; and my possessions to my family." Then he murmured, "I wish to rest in Florence, in the church of Santa Croce with my family."

Tommaso heard that wish and vowed it would be fulfilled. The Pope was determined that Michelangelo should be buried in Rome, and a great funeral was held for him. Somehow Lionardo and Tommaso managed to smuggle the body away, to be sent wrapped in a case of merchandise to Florence.

Michelangelo—sculptor, painter, architect, engineer, and philosopher—lay in state in his home church of Santa Croce while all Florence came to do him honor, to say farewell to the great genius who was their own, a Florentine.

Giorgio Vasari, who wrote the lives of the painters and was working on a biography of Michelangelo while he was alive, wrote after his death:

"The Almighty resolved to send to earth a spirit capable of supreme expression in all the arts, one able to give form to painting, perfection to sculpture, and grandeur to architecture. . . . He decreed that Florence should be the birthplace of this divinely endowed spirit."

INDEX

FOR MORE ABOUT MICHELANGELO

Brion, Marcel. *Michelangelo*. New York: The Greystone Press, 1940.

Lerman, Leo. *Michelangelo: A Renaissance Profile*. New York: Alfred A. Knopf, Inc., 1942.

Papini, Giovanni. *Michelangelo: His Life and His Era*. Translated by Loretta Murnane. New York: E. P. Dutton & Co., 1952.

Rolland, Romain. *Michelangelo*. Translated by Frederick Street. New York: A. & A. Boni, 1935.

Saponaro, Michele. *Michelangelo*. Translated by C. J. Richards. New York: Pellegrini & Cudahy, Inc., 1950.

Stone, Irving. *The Agony and the Ecstasy*. New York: Doubleday & Co., Inc., 1961.

Symonds, John Addington. *The Life of Michelangelo Buonnaroti*. 2 vols. New York: Charles Scribner's Sons, 1911.

Nihil obstat: WALTER H. PETERS, S.T.L., PH.D.
                     Censor Librorum
Imprimatur: ✠   LEO BINZ
                     Archbishop of St. Paul
SEPTEMBER 24, 1962

THE AUTHORS AND THEIR BOOK

ANNE MERRIMAN PECK *was born in Piermont-on-Hudson, New York, and attended art school in New York City. She has been writing and illustrating books for young people all her adult life. Among the more than twenty titles she has had published are* The Pageant of South American History (*David McKay, 1962*), Roundabout Europe (*Harper, 1930*), *and* The March of Arizona History (*Arizona Silhouettes, 1962*). *To gain background material for her work, she has traveled widely in Europe and North and South America. The author lives in Tucson where she gives lectures on juvenile writing to teachers' and librarians' associations and teaches a class on creative writing and illustration at the University of Arizona. In addition to her professional work, she enjoys painting; her art has been exhibited in New York and Tucson.*

FRANK GETLEIN *is a well known art historian and critic. After receiving his Master's degree in Speech and Drama from Catholic University, he held a variety of posts, among them: art critic,* Milwaukee Journal; *movie critic,* The Grail; *television critic,* Today. *He is presently art critic for both the* Washington Sunday Star *and* The New Republic, *as well as Washington correspondent for* Art in America *and* The Burlington Magazine *of London. He has contributed book reviews and articles to many national magazines.*

DOROTHY GETLEIN *received a Bachelor's degree in English from Albertus Magnus College and subsequently became children's librarian for the Boston Public Library.*

THE AUTHORS AND THEIR BOOK

She collaborates with her husband on books and art projects. They are the authors of Christianity in Art, Christianity in Modern Art *(Bruce, 1959, 1961), and* The Bite of the Print *(Clarkson N. Potter, 1962).*

WINGS OF AN EAGLE *(Hawthorn, 1963) was designed by Stefan Salter and completely manufactured by American Book–Stratford Press, Inc. The body type is Linotype Janson, based on the letters of Anton Janson, a Dutch punchcutter who worked between 1660 and 1687.*

A HAWTHORN BOOK

ABOUT CREDO BOOKS

CREDO BOOKS is an important new series of biographies that will appeal to both boys and girls. The subjects of these biographies are Catholic, but their stories are not of their faith so much as how that faith helped them to lead remarkable lives. Past and present will be represented here: a sculptor who left a priceless treasure of art to mankind, or a baseball player who has become an idol to young fans the world over; a movie star who was an idol of a different kind to young and old alike; the president of a South American country who fought against and lost his life to Communist terrorists. Heroes are made by the greatness of the human spirit and all the figures to be portrayed in CREDO BOOKS were great in spirit, courage and effort, no matter what task they took upon themselves.

The authors of these new books have been carefully chosen both for their ability to make biography come alive for young people and their knowledge of their subjects. Such authors as Hugh Ross Williamson, Lon Tinkle, Donald Demarest, Eva K. Betz, Ruth Hume, Frank Kolars and Jack Steffan will be represented.

To give CREDO BOOKS the benefit of their knowledge and experience, an editorial board of distinguished representatives from the fields of education, librarianship and the Catholic press, as well as Hawthorn's own editorial staff, choose both subjects and author for each book in the series.

As an example of the variety of personalities in this new series, you will find the following figures portrayed.

Father Hugh O'Flaherty, by Daniel Madden
Francis X. Ford, by Eva K. Betz
Paderewski, by Ruth and Paul Hume
Thomas More, by Margaret Stanley-Wrench
Joyce Kilmer, by Norah Smaridge
Gregor Mendel, by Gary Webster
Gary Cooper, by Richard Gehman
Col. Carlos Castillo Armas, by Jack Steffan
Ramon Magsaysay, by Gen. Carlos Romulo and Marvin Gray
Mother Katharine Drexel, by Katherine Burton
Tom Dooley, by Terry Morris
Juan Diego, by Lon Tinkle
Mary, Queen of Scots, by Hugh Ross Williamson
Fray Junipero Serra, by Donald Demarest
Charlemagne, by Col. T. N. Dupuy
Pedro Menendez, by Frank Kolars
Genevieve Caulfield, by Elizabeth Young
John McCormack, by Ruth and Paul Hume
Samuel de Champlain, by Charles Morrow Wilson
Louis Braille, by Webb Garrison
Gabriel Richard, by David Abodaher

There is adventure, suspense, excitement and information in CREDO BOOKS.